American Sign Language

© Copyright 2023 - All rights reserved.

The contents of this book may not be reproduced, duplicated, or transmitted without the direct written permission of the author or publisher.

Under no circumstances will the publisher or author be held liable for any damages, recovery, or financial loss due to the information contained in this book. Neither directly nor indirectly.

Legal Notice:

This book is protected by copyright. This book is for personal use only. You may not modify, distribute, sell, use, quote, or paraphrase any part or content of this book without the permission of the author or publisher.

Disclaimer Notice:

Please note that the information contained in this document is for educational and entertainment purposes only. Every effort has been made to present accurate, current, reliable, and complete information. No warranties of any kind are stated or implied. The reader acknowledges that the author is not offering legal, financial, medical, or professional advice. The contents of this book have been taken from various sources. Please consult a licensed professional before attempting any of the techniques described in this book.

By reading this document, the reader agrees that under no circumstances will the author be liable for any direct or indirect loss arising from the use of the information contained in this document, including but not limited to - errors, omissions, or inaccuracies.

Contents

Introduction 3
Chapter 1: What Is ASL 6
Chapter 2: ASL; Emotions, Hands, Faces, And The Body 10
Chapter 3: The Basic Elements Of ASL 13
Chapter 4: Fingerspelling 27
Chapter 5: ASL Alphabet Introduction 29
Chapter 6: Number 47
Chapter 7: The Rules Of ASL Grammar 49
Chapter 8: ASL Classifiers 51
Chapter 9: Common Tenses To Learn In American Sign Language 59
Chapter 10: Commonly Used Signs 61
Chapter 11: Special Tips For ASL 74
Conclusion 81

Introduction

Have you ever met a deaf person who felt you couldn't communicate with them? Does it lead to awkward interactions frequently? Have you ever tried to connect with a deaf person but been unsuccessful? Perhaps you need to learn sign language in order to communicate with your deaf child. There are several reasons why you might have decided to take up this book on American Sign Language.

No spoken language is understood by every human being, and every language has its own set of speakers. Many languages rely on gestures and facial expressions rather than sound to convey meaning. A speaker can readily convey meaning without speaking by using a combination of hand movements, body language, and facial expressions. Sign languages were originally created for the needs of deaf communities, but they have now been expanded for use by persons who are hearing but speechless. There is no global sign language, just as there are hundreds of different spoken languages spoken around the world. There are many distinct kinds of sign languages used in various parts of the world, and each one is unique. One of the most widely used sign languages is American Sign Language (ASL), which is spoken by deaf communities in the United States, Canada, West Africa, and Southeast Asia. American Sign Language (ASL) is a highly developed and widely used language that relies on a combination of hand movements, facial emotions, and body language to transmit meaning.

American Sign Language is the fourth most popular foreign language studied at U.S. universities, which may come as a surprise to some. In the United States alone, ASL is used by at least two million individuals. The primary objective of this book is to facilitate the learning of ASL by anyone interested in expanding their linguistic repertoire. This book will prove to be an all-inclusive guide to American Sign Language thanks to its inclusion of thousands of vocabulary items, numerous drawings, explanations, and gestures to help you practice, as well as some fundamental instances of structures. There are also several questions and exercises included for pupils to test and refine their newfound knowledge.

Learning the fundamentals of a language, be it spoken or signed, is crucial. When interacting with public officials like firefighters, police, and others, this form of communication might be crucial.

To ensure you are always at ease while communicating with those who are deaf or hard of hearing, read this handbook and familiarize yourself with the cultural norms of sign language. Get to know some typical sign expressions, such as those used for saying hello and thank you:

Hello

How do you do?

Where is your home?

Goodbye

Master these and other essential conversational phrases to start feeling more at ease in social situations.

A Brief History Of American Sign Language

Signed languages have existed since languages began, although they weren't recognized as languages until 1817.

In 1815, hearing clergyman Thomas Hopkins Gallaudet toured Europe to study Deaf education. Gallaudet met academics Abbé Roch-Ambroise Cucurron Sicard and Jean Massieu. While studying in England, they invited him to their Paris school. While in Paris, Gallaudet convinced Deaf teacher Laurent Clerc to return to America to educate Deaf students. As they returned to the US, Gallaudet taught Clerc sign language while Clerc taught English. They later created ASL.

In 1817, the two men established what is today known as the School for the Deaf as the Hartford Asylum for the Study and Education of Deaf and Dumb People in Hartford, a city in Connecticut. "Dumb" is slang for those who are unable to speak. This made Clerc became a pioneering Deaf educator in France. ASL was not recognized as an official language for Deaf people until 1965 when historical linguist William Stokoe published a book establishing its structure and grammar. Gallaudet University English instructor Stokoe observed ASL and student interactions. He studied and wrote about ASL, believing it was a true language with syntax and organization. His theory changed ASL's history, despite criticism. Since then, the number of Americans and Canadians learning ASL has increased. In 2019, Newsweek projected that one million people used ASL as their primary language.

Chapter 1: What is ASL

The majority of deaf and hard-of-hearing people in the US and Canadians use American Sign Language, sometimes referred to as ASL or Ameslan, as their main means of interaction. It's estimated that up to two million Americans are native speakers of American Sign Language (ASL). It combines a number of sign languages, including French, British, and regional sign languages from throughout the world.

The idea that American Sign Language is just adapted English for the deaf and hard of hearing is one of the most pervasive misunderstandings about the language. It is a unique language with its own syntax, vocabulary, idioms, and cultural norms. In linguistics, sign language (ASL) is studied separately from other languages. Since it incorporates hand gestures and visual expression, American Sign expression is a genuinely distinctive method of communication. An ASL user communicates by combining facial expressions, body language, gestures, palm orientations, and hand shapes in place of speech. It could take a lot of time and effort to learn the nuances of this type of communication.

There are signs in this language that are completely opaque, partially transparent, or wholly transparent. Clear signs are simple to comprehend, especially for people who are still learning the language. Transparent signals can be understood by non-native speakers after the message has been sent. On the other side, it can be difficult for someone who does not utilize sign language to understand the meaning of an opaque sign. The majority of ASL signs are opaque, which is essential for effective communication.

Those who are interested in learning ASL can do it in a number of ways. Many secondary and postsecondary schools offer American Sign Language courses to help students satisfy their requirements for foreign language studies. If you want to learn ASL more haphazardly, there are a number of internet resources that might help you get started.

Beyond interacting with the deaf and hard of hearing, American Sign Language is utilized for a number of other applications.

Why should you become proficient in American Sign Language?

Words and phrases in American Sign Language (ASL) are formed through the use of hand gestures, body language, and facial emotions. About 500,000 people in the United States are native speakers, making it the third most spoken language there. Publications on pedagogical practices and methods of manual communication date back to at least 1817. Even before he had a chance to study ASL himself, Frelinghuysen gave a public demonstration of the language in 1860. American Sign Language (ASL) is a dynamic language that has been affected by others, including French Sign Language (LSF). There are various regional variations of ASL because the language is not standardized.

Deaf and hard-of-hearing infants and toddlers have been found to benefit from learning sign language. Adults and older children can benefit from learning sign language by improving their lip-reading, speech-articulation, and communicative abilities. Equally essential to communication as spoken language is sign language. Those who happen to be deaf or hard of listening may not be able to understand you without it.

Evidence also suggests that teaching youngsters sign language can facilitate their linguistic growth. Children with ADD/ADHD can benefit from this rule since it prevents them from engaging in activities that might otherwise distract them from their schoolwork, such as playing with other students. Learning American Sign Language vocabulary can serve as a stepping stone to learning other languages, and it's a terrific way to communicate effectively on its own or in combination with spoken language.

If you want to learn any other language, this is the "key" to do so. Hence studying ASL is highly recommended. Each sign in sign language has a specific meaning, and students of the language gain a practical understanding of those meanings as they study the language. It's the linguistic equivalent of the Rosetta Stone. You can learn additional languages, like Spanish, French, or German, once you know the fundamentals of sign language and a few words.

Sign language is utilized in the medical industry, as well as in the education of the deaf and hard of hearing and the acquisition of new languages. Sign language is used at over a hundred different hospitals and schools across the United States to aid patients and pupils in their recovery from illness and injury. In order to get a proper interpretation of the signs being employed, patients or pupils may have to debate with the doctors or nurses.

One of the most prevalent motivations for learning a new language nowadays is to better understand the culture of the people who speak it. Though it has been around since 1817, sign language does not get nearly enough use. I encourage anyone who has a friend or family member learning ASL or who is interested in learning it themselves to pick up the language. Learning is very satisfying and beneficial in many ways.

As the world grows more interconnected, knowing sign language might be useful while visiting a foreign country. Since American Sign Language (ASL) is understood by people of all linguistic backgrounds, you'll have no trouble communicating with your travel companions, the hotel staff, the taxi drivers, and anyone else you encounter along the way.

People who are deaf or hard of hearing have their own language—sign language. It's a way of communicating using body language and expressions rather than words.

Despite sign language's longevity, it is not utilized nearly as frequently as it should be, leaving many deaf people out of everyday conversations.

Researchers in the field of linguistics believe that the use of signs and symbols for communication precedes written language, which explains the quick development of sign language. The deaf and the hard of hearing have access to a visual form of communication thousands of years ago, according to famous thinkers like Socrates.

Numerous sign languages are in use across the globe. More people in Europe speak BSL and FSL than any other language. On the other side, American Sign Language has a larger user base in the Americas. Multiple sign languages exist, although none are used everywhere.

Learning sign language is useful for more than only those who have trouble communicating verbally. This language is useful in situations where verbal communication is difficult or impossible. The capacity to communicate with hand gestures is extremely useful in dangerous situations.

Sign language is not simple to learn on one's own, but it should be used more frequently anyway. Even if you may see signing during the news on a few different channels, it's most useful during live broadcasts.

It has been said that learning a new language, particularly one as visually and tactilely taxing as sign language, is a fantastic opportunity to broaden one's horizons and put one's skills to the test. You will be better able to take in and interpret your surroundings once you've learned this visual and spatial language.

Should Sign Language Be Taught?

Students who study ASL are more likely to develop compassion for the world's 360 million deaf and hard-of-hearing persons. If you take the time to learn American Sign Language (ASL), you'll be able to better interact with deaf individuals and promote greater understanding and acceptance of ASL among the hearing population. The number of people who rely solely on sign language to express themselves is growing rapidly. More than 70 million people throughout the world communicate via sign language. A person's professional and academic prospects may both benefit from their school offering sign language classes. The majority of experts agree that sign language is among the quickest and easiest languages to learn. Learning sign language has more advantages than learning any other foreign language. If learning sign language makes you uncomfortable, you should get help from a qualified professional. About 26 different hand gestures are needed for fluent communication in American Sign Language. To begin learning this new concept, a deaf person would need supplementary assistance.

Realizing How Beneficial Sign Language Can Be

There are many cognitive advantages to learning a sign language, and improved spatial transformation ability is just one of them. Those that put in the effort to learn a sign language have been shown to fare better than those who don't. Students in mainstream education who learn ASL will have an easier time relating to and conversing with their deaf and hard-of-hearing peers. Sign language is extremely useful for the deaf and hard of hearing, but hearing individuals can also gain a lot from studying it. Everyone should be able to learn sign language if that's the goal.

Chapter 2: ASL; Emotions, Hands, Faces, and the Body

Introduction

In American Sign Language (ASL), there are five (5) core components for communicating with the deaf community. Here they are, from most to least crucial:

1. Make direct eye contact

2. Expression on the face

3. Nonverbal cues

4. A wiggle of the mouth

5. Gesturing using hands

6. Norms of behaviour

Make direct eye contact

Without maintaining eye contact, communication with the deaf is difficult. If you look away, you're done talking to that person. This is typically taken as an indication of rudeness or anger and can cause great distress among the deaf community.

It's best to avoid directly interrupting a deaf person during a conversation if at all feasible. If you can't, you should "duck" or bend over (assuming you don't have any physical limitations) and say "excuse me" without drawing the deaf person's visual attention. It's impolite to pass between two people who are communicating sign language without first attracting their attention, but it's much more impolite to call out to them as you're passing! Do not do that.

It is crucial for hearing individuals to realize how important eye contact is to deaf people. In class, a hearing student can take notes while listening to the instructor. They need not constantly search. However, a deaf student must rely on a sign language interpreter or watch the lecturer sign in order to follow along with the lecture.

Expression on the face

Explanations of adverbs, adjectives, superlatives, and intensities can be found in facial expressions. Pronouns can also be shown through head movements to or away from an individual. The speaker is able to comment on the behaviors of others and communicate their viewpoint in regard to those acts through the use of facial expressions. For instance, if your younger brother has a larger quantity of chocolate ice cream than you have, your facial expressions will convey that you are perplexed and asking, "Why does he have more ice cream than me?"

Nonverbal cues

Whatever is going on in the world around us, our bodies respond to it. We get out of the way of whatever makes us feel threatened or unsafe. We gravitate toward things that pique our interest or captivate our attention. Observing the relatively insignificant motions of another person's body can provide us with a wealth of information regarding that person's state of mind. All of these kinesthetic cues are considered part of the entire communication process in American Sign Language (ASL).

A wiggle of the mouth

The movements of the mouth do not necessarily indicate what is being said in English. It provides a visual representation of the various dimensions that are being discussed. For instance, if the signer is referring to extremely enormous objects, they might puff out their cheeks while blowing air out of their mouths. Or, when they are referring to a somewhat insignificant item, such as some dental floss, they may draw their lips together or have the air sucked into their cheeks.

Gesturing using hands

The hand gestures used in formal sign language are inextricable from the other factors discussed. The whole contributes to the seamlessness of the exchange. Keep in mind that ASL is not based on English words but on space and visual perception. When two or more ASL signs are strung together to form a phrase, it is NOT a literal translation of two or more English words. Many of us use English as our first language, so learning American Sign Language will need some work on your behalf. When combined with facial expressions, body language, and other contextual cues, ASL signs can convey a wide range of meanings.

Learning sign language requires a person to be open to the visual and physical aspects of communication. Most hearing individuals learn early on to hide their true feelings and rely instead on carefully chosen words to express their meaning. Among the many insults a hearing person can level at a deaf person, "stone face" is among the worst. When someone signs with a stone face, they don't display any expression on their face. Those who are deaf find this extremely irritating. They may become irrational or angry because they cannot read your expressions. As you add more signatures and revisions, you stop caring so much about getting everything just right. You can "chill out" and enjoy the full range of feelings that come with effective communication. You can improve your signing skills by learning to recognize and work with your feelings.

Norms of behaviour

Hearing persons use their hearing and voices to exchange English words and phrases. Sign language is used by the deaf community as a means of communication. Keep in mind that words are only symbols used in language. What matters is HOW we employ these signs of language in our interactions with one another.

Images are essential for visual communication. American Sign Language (ASL) is a very evocative language. Letters and sounds make up the alphabet, which defines English. Expression and gesture are the "alphabet" of American Sign Language. In conclusion, the English language has both words and visuals that explain signs.

Because of your hearing, you use language in all of these areas. We use words to communicate with others and with ourselves. If you really want to understand what ASL can do, you have to forget about words and just look at the pictures. Experience the physical act of signing in order to visualize it.

To practice, try this: Imagine a nice or lovely time or place. A place where one feels good about themselves, such as a vacation home, favorite spot, peaceful library, or similar. Imagine and explain in detail the sights, sounds, and overall atmosphere of this happy place. Most people find this to be a trying and unpleasant experience. Why? You aren't used to contemplation without words.

The "seeing mode" or mindset is essential for fluency in American Sign Language. Instead of relying on English descriptions, students of American Sign Language must learn to interpret visual cues and physical gestures. You then begin to think through the use of nonverbal cues. Despite the vast differences between ASL and English, it is fair to state that the deaf are bilingual.

Chapter 3: The Basic Elements of ASL

Introduction

As you may have guessed by now, the deaf employ a kind of sign language called American Sign Language (ASL), which is derived from natural motions that have been reduced to symbol signs over time. These symbol signs are derived from a synthesis of preexisting American Sign Language signs with spoken movement and expressiveness. A sign is a gesture, and a gesture is a symbol. This is analogous to how sounds become words, which become sentences in any language.

The four basic parts of ASL signing are:

-- Handshape

-- Palm orientation

-- Hand orientation

-- Placement

An essential research question from cognitive psychologists Laura Ann Petitto and Paula F. Marentette of McGill University in Montreal. They discovered that deaf infants engage in hand babble in the same way as hearing infants engage in voice babble. The method of studying a new tongue is the same for both. Deaf infants, like their hearing counterparts, often make up words and string together unrelated sounds when first learning to communicate. Babbling, according to these researchers, is a representation of the abstract linguistic framework shared by many languages that allows for the efficient processing of a large number of signs, whether verbal or nonverbal.

Learning the meaning and use of these four components is the first step in becoming fluent in American Sign Language. The various components of signing can add to, modify, or otherwise affect the meanings of ASL signs in the same way that prefixes and suffixes can change the meanings of English words. So, to break it down,

Handshape

Understanding the significance of the various hand forms is crucial. The alphabet and several number signs provide the basis for many of the handshapes used in the signs you may have "picked up" on your travels. There are many other hand gestures mentioned, including the fully extended "C" hand, and the tightly clasped "claw" palm (the "C" palm with the fingertips curled in), the extended finger ("1" hand), the open "O" hand, a fist ("S" hand), and the either closed or open "5" hand. Likewise to how different combinations of sounds may form a new English word, the meaning of a set of hand gestures can change depending on how they are utilized. These morphemes which are little grammatical units that create words or significant chunks of any word that can't be broken down into smaller portions, are hand shapes that are similar to sounds.

This implies that the meaning of a form may shift even while the handshapes remain same; this occurs when the palm orientation, hand movement, or hand location are altered. You can see this in action with the placards indicating who owns what.

Yours

Ours 1

Ours 2

Ours 3

Mine

Signing "yours" involves a palm-outward motion and a hand placed in front of the face, as if to say, "It's yours." The sign meaning "ours" is made by moving the hands in a circle, palms out, and placing them wherever the signer and the other person are together; "It's ours." All of the hand's movements, palms, and placements for "mine" face the person who is signing, as if to say, "It's my own." The "5" hand form, closed, is used in all of those symbols.

People who have become proficient in sign language may create stunning musical works by modifying several aspects of a single sign. This implies that the signals used in signing shouldn't only communicate the content of the words in the English phrase, but should also be chosen for their aesthetic value. Using literary tropes like rhyme, stress, and soft/hard consonants to evoke a certain feeling in the reader or listener is analogous to this process. Signers employ ASL's fundamental components—signs, facial expressions respectively, and body language—to create beautiful communication.

Palm Orientation

The signs for "yours," "mine," and "ours" demonstrate how the palm of the hand may be oriented to convey possession. A good gesture is made when the palm faces inward or is facing upward, whereas a negative gesture is made when the palm faces away from the body or is facing downward. We will demonstrate the importance of palm orientation in ASL conversational structure.

Know / Don't Know 1

Don't Know 2

Don't Know 3

Let's take a look at what we do and don't already know:

The "3" hand gesture is used in both situations. By placing the palm of your hand on the right side of your forehead (if that you're right-handed; on the other side if that you're left-handed) and tapping the middle of your temple with the leading edges of your index fingers, you may communicate, "I am familiar with something." The "I don't know about this" hand gesture is made by turning the hand's palm so that the fingertips face the forehead and then rotating the hand so that the palms and hand face aside from the head (while the fingers continue to point up). The head is simultaneously shaking no. Because of this difference in significance, the palms must be oriented differently.

We need to experience the sign, not just duplicate it, which might be difficult for hearing individuals. Developing this sensitivity will help us with both the expressive (using ASL to communicate with others) and receptive (reading the signs of other deaf people) aspects of ASL. Perform the symbols for "yours," "my," "ours," "know," & "have no idea" while in front of a mirror. Make sure you practice the appropriate expression of the face, mouth activity, and movement of the body for every gesture as you learn it. Use your spontaneous gestures as a guide to improve the clarity of each sign you learn.

Hand Movement

A sign's connotation may be subtly altered depending on how the hands are moved when performing it. It is possible to describe a signature just by observing the movements of the signer's hands. The larger motions indicate an open or vast space, while the smaller moves indicate a tight or compact space. Signs that are created either very slowly or very swiftly give off the impression that there is no haste or rush. If the sign consists of repetitive gestures - or if the motions themselves are repeated numerous times - then this signifies that the activity has been repeated. On the other hand, if a sign is performed in a circular motion, this indicates that the activity is ongoing.

Work 1

Work 2

Depend 1

Depend 2

Placement

In body language, signals that are near to the body relate to the person doing the signing, and signs that are farther out from the person indicate to another person or entity. Therefore, placement (or position) is used in interactions to construct pronouns like as "myself," "yours," ourselves, "him," "her," "that thing," and so on, as well as noun subjects.

You

Me

Us 1

Us 2

Us 3

He/She/It 1

He/She/It 2

The dominant fingers pointing finger is used as the pronoun handshape. If the person to whom the pronoun refers is present, the pointer moves to that person. Pointing one's finger is considered rude by those with normal hearing. However, the deaf community generally accepts and values sign language as a substantial and time-saving means of communication. In reality, pointing fingers serves several purposes in American Sign Language (ASL) and is an integral aspect of the language's grammar. If you want to communicate about a "table" or "house," for instance, you might sign or spell "table" and then point to the object in question. After the first mention, if you continue talking about the table, the deaf person will understand that you are only pointing at the table.

You sign "student" #1 and point to the right while you're at home telling your sibling about your day at school. Then you gesture left and write "student" again, indicating student number 2. Neither classmate came homes with you, and neither is anybody in your residence space; what you've done is set up a visual reference for your tale by placing them to your right and left. So, when you narrate the narrative, you swivel your head and gesture to the proper position to emphasize whatever Student #1 said or did. In addition, you will indicate with a leftward nod and point whatever Student #2 stated or did. "Pronoun placement" is the term used in American Sign Language for this placement.

Variety Is the Spice of Life

Conversation is rich in detail; it's the spice that brightens the everyday. Learn how to use descriptive language to name people and convey your thoughts and feelings in this chapter. Furthermore, certain splashes of color will be used for dramatic effect.

Human Characteristics

To put it simply, human beings are not all the same. If everyone were exactly the same, life on Earth would be very dull. A person's height, eye color, and hair color are all examples of distinguishing features. These qualities are often used while describing other people. There are conventions for characterizing persons in sign language.

People are often described in a certain sequence, with their gender coming first. After that, we move on to other physical characteristics like height, hair color, and cut. The description may be expanded to include the person's unique characteristics if they exist. The size of one's grin, the color of one's eyes, or one's mannerisms are all examples of physical traits that might be memorable.

Using your index finger, you may make the sign for "face" by tracing a circle around your face. The sign for "hair" is made by touching or caressing one's own hair. A person's hairdo may be described by mimicking that person's hairstyle. Perhaps you've used mime to refer to a person who has a beard or mustache. Sign language is greatly complemented by the use of natural gestures. It is acceptable practice to use them. In fact, you should feel free to communicate yourself via non-verbal means.

The following few paragraphs will teach you some basic sign language for describing yourself and others via the use of color, clothes, and mood.

Color My World

The easiest technique to memorize color signs is to learn them in sets based on place (that is, wherever on the body the signs are signed). All of the face-signed hues are listed below:

- Colors like pink and red may be created on the lips.

- The tan and brown hair on the side of the face is brushed.

- Squeezing an orange on the cheek. Keep in mind that the symbol for "orange" might also indicate something else. The hand on the face suggests the color orange, while the hand near the mouth suggests orange juice.

- The eyebrow becomes completely black.

Chapter 4: Fingerspelling

Finger spelling

As the name implies, "finger spelling" is the process in which one utilizes one's fingers to stand in for each letter of a standard alphabet. Because it allows users to hand spell the initials of people, things, and places that don't have a conventional sign, it's an essential tool for signers. The sign for "tree" is used in most languages of sign as an illustration. However, it's possible they don't have a term for "oak," in which case you'd have to finger spell the letters o-a-k to make your point.

American Sign Language relies heavily on fingerspelling. Although the vocabulary of sign language is vast, many English words remain unsigned or are represented by acronyms. To emphasize a specific word, one can fingerspell it. Names and locations will be fingerspelled using the knowledge you have of the alphabet.

The criteria for fingerspelling:

- Please restrain yourself from reaching up or reaching out.

- Instead of pronouncing each letter as you type it, speak the complete word out loud.

- Accuracy is more crucial than speed.

- Keep your correspondence consistent in tone.

- Except when marking the letters G or H, your hand should be held in a forward position.

The 26 letters of the alphabet are used to spell out words via finger spelling. Use of fingerspelling is uncommon among ASL signers. It is commonly used to convey place names and coordinates in the absence of standardized signage.

Try acting out the word, indicating at a certain thing, miming it, or drawing it if you don't know the sign for it. To rephrase, don't try to fingerspell something on a sign if you have no idea what it says. When no sign exists for a given word, fingerspelling is used instead. In ASL, fingerspelling is only necessary in the following situations:

Genuine place names and city names; legitimate product names and movie titles.

You should try your hand at using your fingers to spell three-letter words now that you know the manual alphabet. Spelling bee games are a great way to sharpen your vocabulary and your spelling skills. As you move from letter to letter, you'll train your fingers to be more dexterous. Later, you and a fingerspelling pal can engage in some friendly competition at a spelling bee. Why don't you settle down already? Try to find one, and remember that in order to teach, you must first learn.

The rules for competing in the spelling bee with a buddy are as follows. Everyone takes turns picking a word from a list and fingerspelling it. The receiver is responsible for sending back the word with the right fingerspelling. After that, we double-check every single word. Keep going until all the words are printed using your fingers. You might want to think about upping the difficulty level. Compile a new set of 50 nouns and verbs. The ideal length for these words is four or five characters. The pronunciation bee game can be played indefinitely by just increasing the length and difficulty of the words.

Fingerspelled Loan Signs

The utilization of "loan signs" and shorthand written with the fingerspelling alphabet is yet another way in which the strokes of the traditional alphabet are put to use. "Loan signs" contain distinctive trends and gestures. They often have between two and five characters, which means that they are terms that are used frequently. These words are all constructed and fashioned in a variety of different patterns, such as these:

- Fingerspelling "bus" involves moving from the letter "B" to the letter "S" in a vertical and downward motion.
- Fingerspelling "all" involves moving from left to right while utilizing the characters "A" through "L" in a continuous motion.
- The word "dog" may be spelled utilizing your fingers by clicking the characters "D" through "G" in succession.
- Fingerspelling the word "Apt" involves a swift downward and upward flicking of the wrist to form the letters "A," "P," and "T," respectively.
- Fingerspelling the word "refrigerator" involves writing the characters "R," "E," and "F" in a downward-facing vertical motion.

The loan signs that you just signed have been constructed over time and have shown themselves to be an efficient means of signing these phrases. You just used them to sign a loan agreement.

These loan signals have been acceptable signs in their loan format throughout the course of time, which has also contributed to their appearance and movement. Keep in mind, however, that in addition to the signs shown above, each of these terms also has a conventional entire sign in American Sign Language.

Chapter 5: ASL Alphabet Introduction

The alphabet has the biggest role in knowing ASL. This is because ASL often uses terms like "C hand" or "N hand," etc. When it comes to having a deaf person who can comprehend you, you're "in trouble" if you don't know the C hand.

Considering the ASL alphabet's importance, it is necessary to note that it is also VERY challenging to learn and retain. Therefore, unless you're a language genius (whose memory of languages, word meanings, etc., is incredibly easy), you would retain this information by simple repetition.

Now for the details: A number of letters (and words) have a similar hand form but vary depending on whether they are placed on your body or in the air. Or their hand shapes are completely different, yet they use distinct hand digits.

The following are some instances, which are also mentioned in this section:

 A and S= The fingers of both the letters A and S are curled into the palm. The thumb is placed to the side in the A hand, while it is folded over the fingers in the S hand to form a "fist."

D and F= In the D hand, the thumb and middle finger are in contact, and the index finger is facing upward. The ring and pinky fingers are also curled and parallel to the middle finger.

G and Q= these two represented by the straight-out index and thumb of the G hand. The same digits are used on the Q hand, except they point downward. The middle, ring, and pinky fingers are curled into the palm in both instances.

The Letter A

T

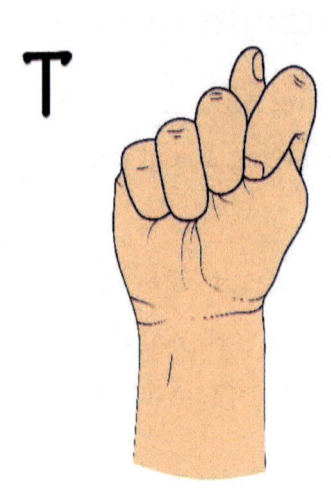

Making a modified fist allows you to create the letter A; however, this fist is different since the thumb is positioned on the side of the bent index finger rather than over the front of the fingers.

SECTION 5-3

The Letter B

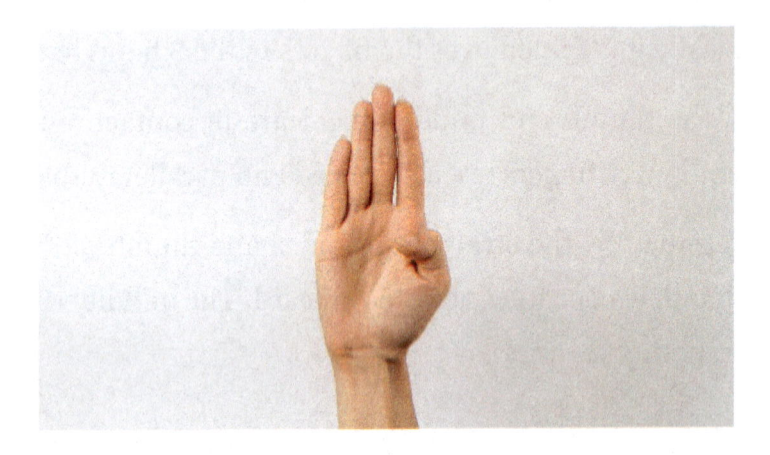

The right side of the thumb (this ebook assumes you're using the right hand; use the left hand if you're a "southpaw") contacts the palm near the fingers when the hand is held with the palm facing out and the thumb crossed over, bent (at the joint).

The Letter C

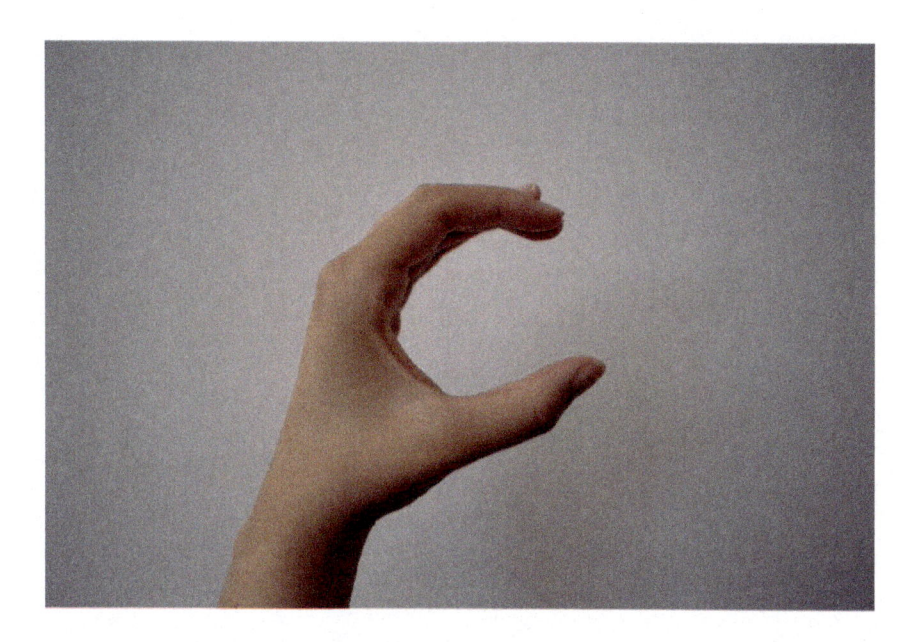

The letter C is created by spacing the bent finders and cupping the hand. To do this, stretch the bent thumb forward while bending the fingers forward.

The Letter D

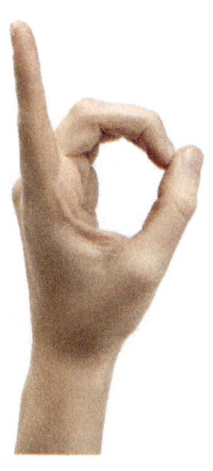

The right (or left) index finger is extended to create the letter D, and the middle finger is bent to contact the tip of the thumb. The ring and pinky fingers are then bent to match the middle finger.

The Letter E

The fingernail tips of the index, middle, and ring fingers should contact the front of the inwardly bent thumb to create the letter E. This is accomplished by bending or "squeezing" the fingers together. To align with the other fingers, the pinky finger is bent.

The Letter F

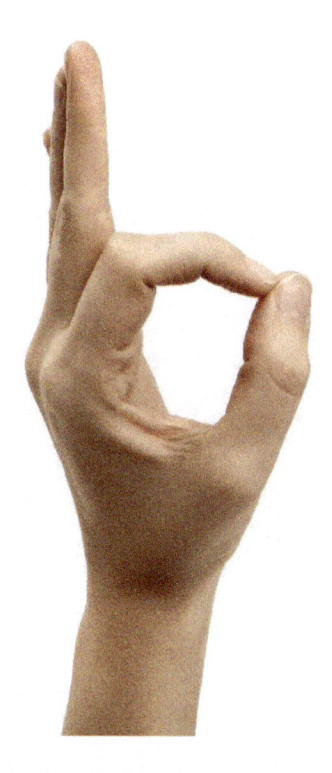

Making the "OK" gesture entails bending the index finger forward and extending the thumb forward until the tips of both contacts create the letter F. It is best if the middle, ring, and pinky are all perfectly straight.

The Letter G

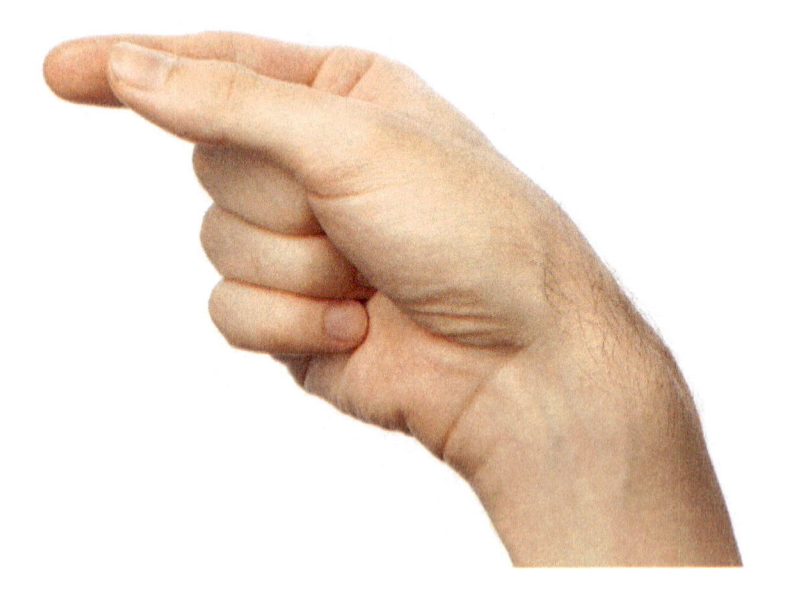

The middle, ring, and pinky fingers are folded into the palm to make the letter G, and the index and thumb are then extended outward (away from the body).

The letter H

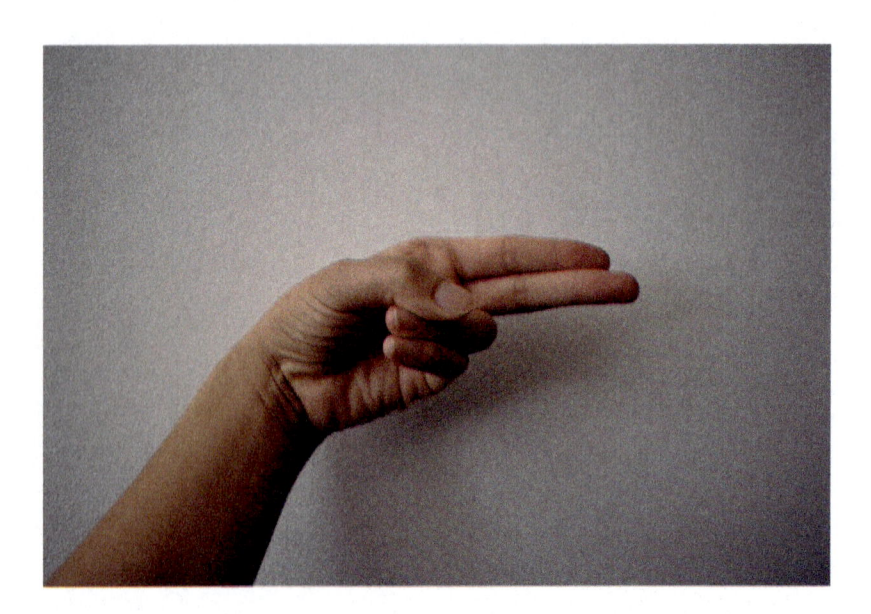

The ring and pinky fingers are held down with the thumb while the index and middle fingers are extended from the body and squeezed together to create the letter H.

The Letter I

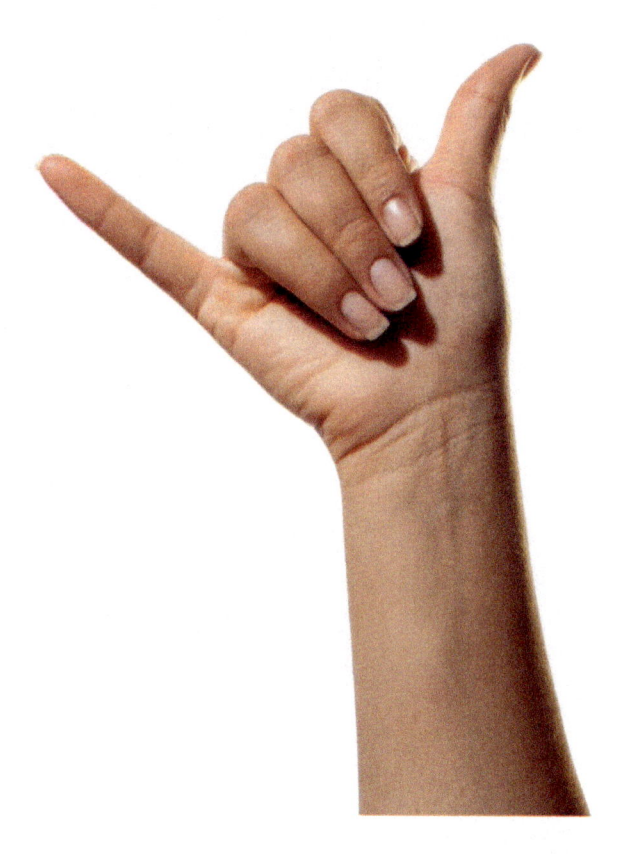

The pinky finger is held up as the thumb presses down on the index, middle, and ring fingers to make the letter I.

The Letter J [1 of 2]

The "I hand" is initially made at about a 45-degree angle to create the letter J (1).

The Letter J [2 of 2]

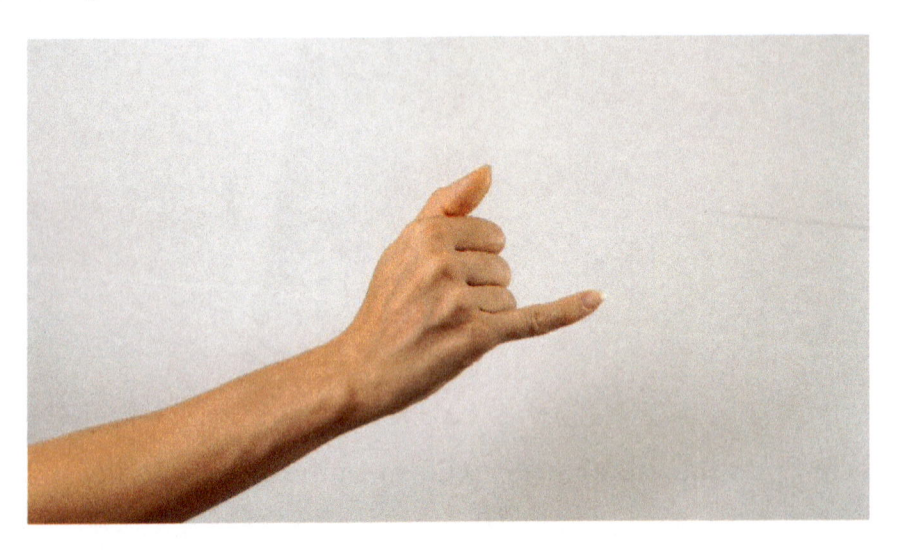

The letter J (2) is continued by taking the hand used to form the letter J (1) and swinging it to the left. Hence, the pinky finger goes from the right side pointing up (with the thumb, folded fingers, and palm pointing to the left at a 45-degree angle), then swinging it to the left so the thumb, folded fingers, and palm are pointing toward the body at a 45-degree angle. This completes the letter.

The Letter K

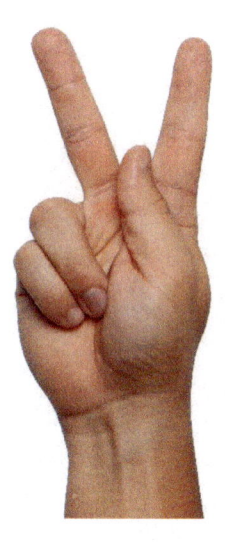

When forming the letter K, the index finger is held up, the middle finger is pointed straight ahead, and the thumb is pressed on the left side of the middle finger between the two joints. This creates the letter K. Meanwhile, the middle and ring fingers are forced into the palm.

The Letter L

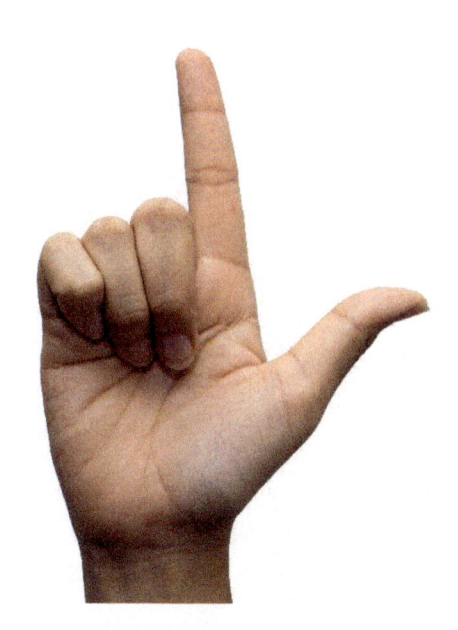

When forming the letter L, the index finger is positioned to point upwards, the thumb is positioned to point outwards, and the middle, ring, and pinky fingers are positioned to curl into the palm.

The Letter M

The letter M may be made by bringing all of the fingers into the palm and bending them. The next step is to grab the thumb, elevate the index, middle, and ring fingers, and then slide the thumb between the ring and pinky fingers on the palm.

The Letter N

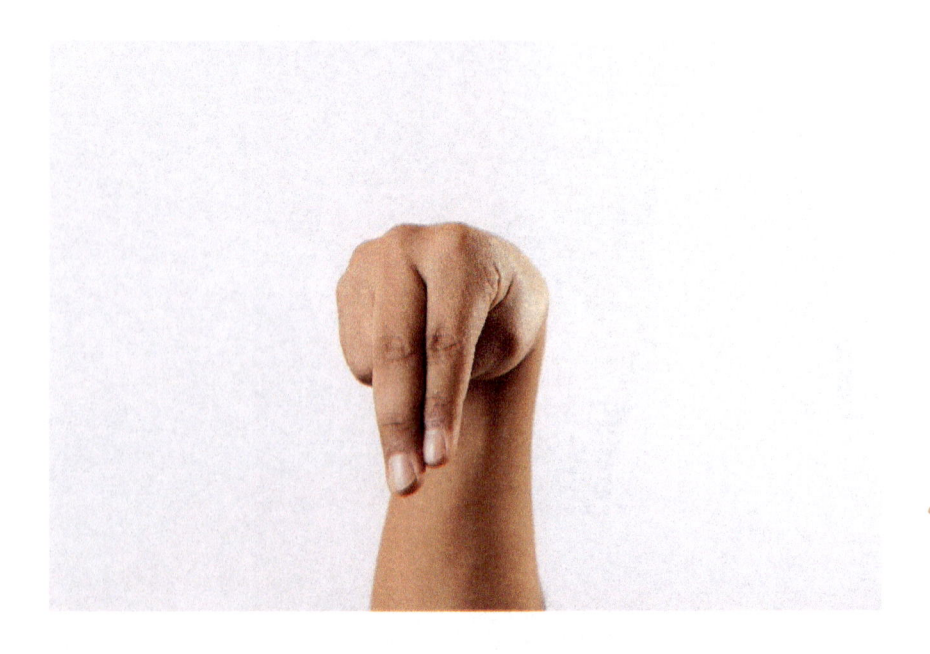

The letter N may be made by bringing all of the fingers into the palm and bending them. The next step is to grab the thumb, elevate the index and middle fingers, and then move the thumb to position it between the middle and ring fingers on the palm of the hand.

The Letter O

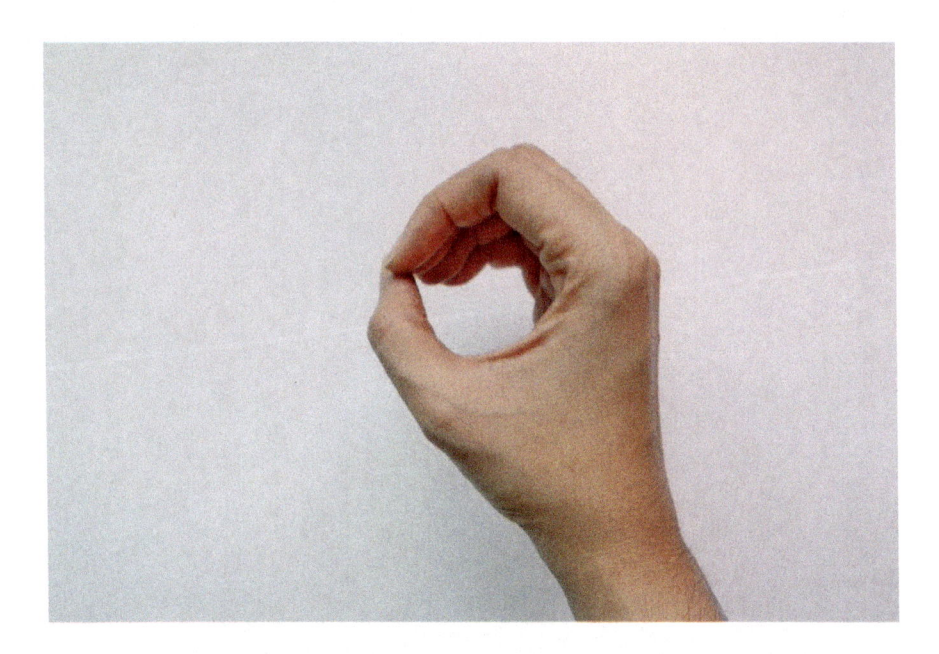

To make the letter O, curl all your fingers into a tight "claw" hand while bringing your thumb forward and into contact with your index and middle fingers. This creates the shape of the letter O.

The Letter P

The letter P is made by extending the index finger forward, pointing the middle finger down at a 45-degree angle, and touching the left side of the middle finger between the two joints with the thumb. This position causes the thumb to contact the left side of the middle finger. The ring and pinky fingers are rolled into the palm during this time.

The Letter Q

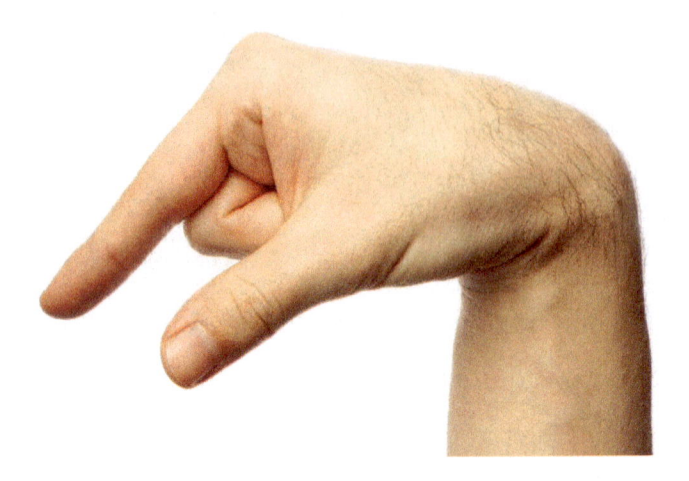

To write the letter Q, fold your middle, ring, and pinky fingers into the palm of your hand. Next, extend your index finger and thumb downwards at a 45-degree angle.

The Letter R

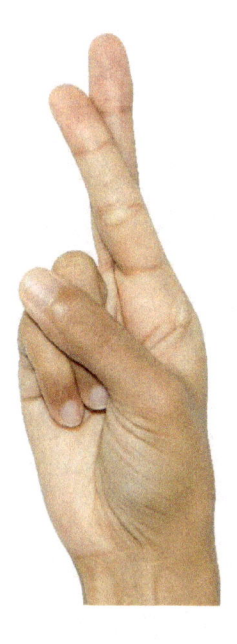

R

The letter R may be made by making the "good luck" gesture, which consists of extending the index and middle fingers upward while simultaneously "hugging" the index finger with the middle finger by placing it behind it. At the same time, the little finger and the ring finger are kept in a pressed position by the thumb.

The Letter S

To make the letter S, make a modified "fist" hand as follows: all the fingers are curled into the palm, and the thumb is crossed over and pushed against the curled fingers.

The Letter T

To make the letter T, one must bring the tips of all of one's fingers together into the palm of one's hand. The next step is to take the thumb, elevate the index finger, and place it between the middle and index fingers on the palm side of the hand.

The Letter U

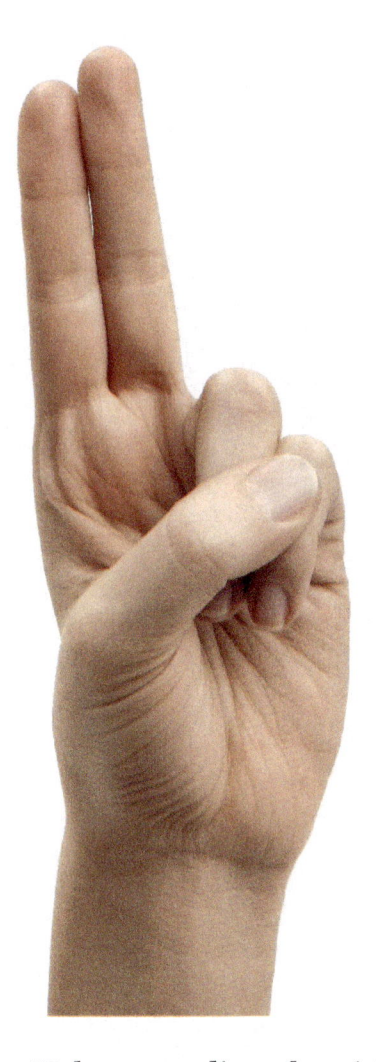

It is possible to make the letter U by extending the right index and middle fingers and subsequently bending the right ring and pinky fingers such that the tips of those fingers contact the tip of the right thumb.

The Letter V

The letter V may be made by making the "peace hand" in the following manner: extending the right index and middle fingers and then splitting them; bending the right ring and pinky fingers so that they both touch the tip of the thumb; and last, separating the right index and middle fingers.

The Letter W

W may be made by extending the index, middle, and ring fingers on the right hand, then separating them. Additionally, the pinky finger should be bent to meet the tip of the thumb.

The Letter X

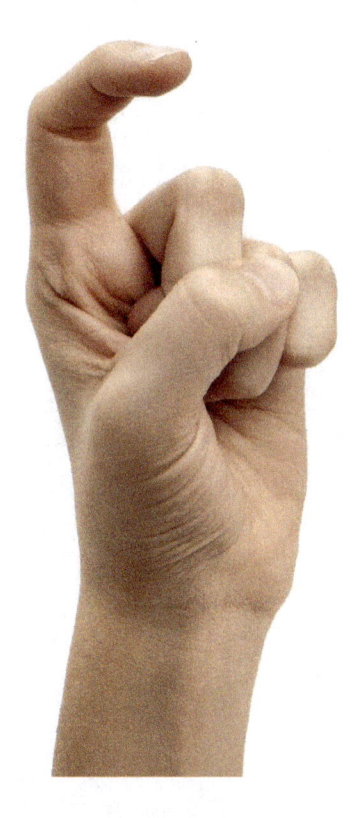

To make an X hand, curl all of the fingers into the palm of your hand, and bring the right side or back of your thumb into touch with the middle finger alone or the middle and ring fingers (depending on how flexible your hand is). After that, the index finger's top and middle joints are flexed forward.

The Letter Y

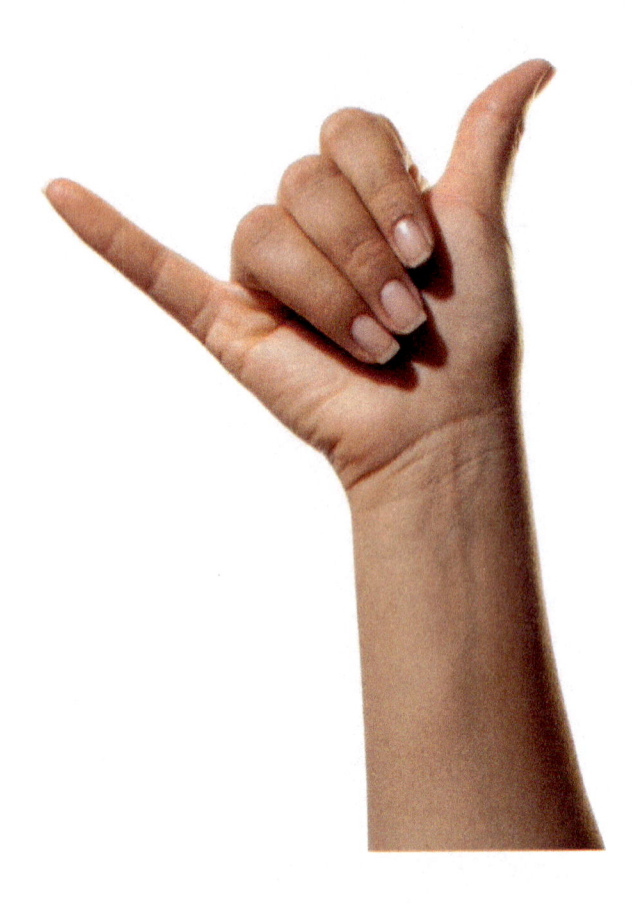

To make a Y hand, you should maintain your thumb and pinky finger extended as you curl your index, middle, and ring fingers into the palm of your hand.

The Z Hand [1 of 4]

The "pointing at someone hand" is the first step in making the Z hand. This hand is produced by pointing your index finger toward the upper right side of your body.

The Z Hand [2 of 4]

To continue the Z hand, you will need to make a body crossing from the upper right to the top left of your body.

The Z Hand [3 of 4]

Continue the Z hand by pointing from the upper left to the lower right of your torso (imagine this as the shape of "half an X").

The Z Hand [4 of 4]

After that, you should point from the lower right to the lower left of your body to complete the Z hand.

Chapter 6: Number

In ASL, counting is done entirely with one hand. If presenting just the numbers 1 through 5, the palm should be facing inward. Like numerous other number designations, they are carried out with the palm of the hand facing forward when employed in a sequence of numbers. The 11–15 range is always marked with the hand pointing inward.

Once you know how to represent numbers from 1 through 30, as well as HUNDRED, THOUSAND, and MILLION, you can easily create any other number using only these fundamental symbols. To learn about other differences and subtleties in the signature of numbers, see more in-depth sources.

Number Basics

In American Sign Language, the dominant hand is utilized to create the numbers.

Signing the first two digits is all that's required after the number 26. Another sign is unnecessary. The palm should be pointing outward when signing a string of numbers such as a phone number.

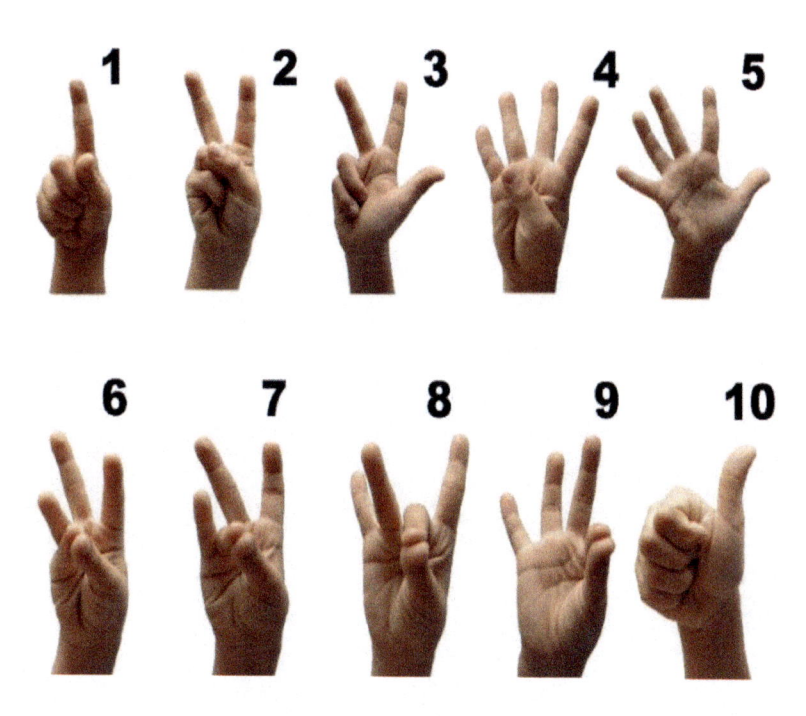

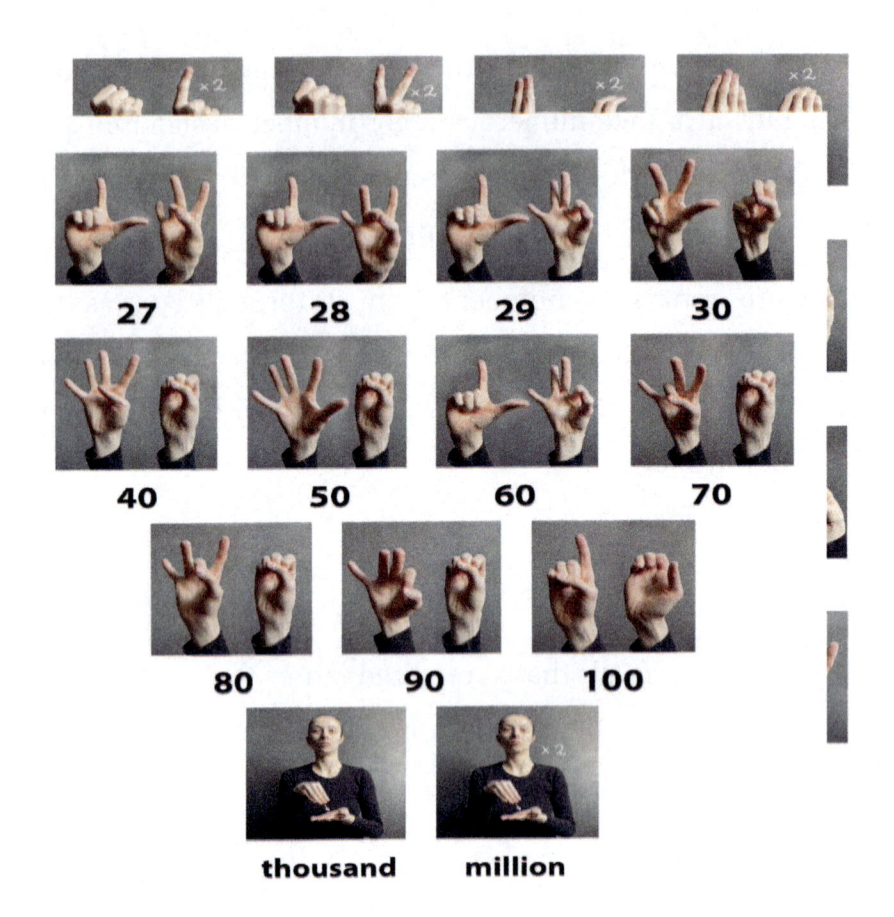

American Sign Language

27 28 29 30

40 50 60 70

80 90 100

thousand million

Chapter 7: The rules of ASL grammar

Here are some basic rules of ASL grammar that will help you communicate more effectively with the Deaf population.

1) Do not try to apply English grammar principles to ASL; the two languages have different grammatical systems. For instance, in ASL, you can't just say "yes" by nodding your head up and down.

2) Two rapid head shakes mean "no" and one gradual shaking means "yes" when asked a yes/no question. Case in point: the age-old inquiry, "Are you hungry?" (Meaning "no") The correct answer is "no."

3) Use the same two shakes as in the previous section, but this time say "y" for "yes" instead. Take the question "Is that your son?" as an illustration. Because it is, is the answer for an affirmative.

4) When substituting a noun or pronoun in a sentence, utilize the word's final letter.

5) The shape of your hands when signing the letter S also serves to construct the plural.

6) To indicate ownership, place the ASL sign "AT" (made with a particular handshape) in front of the item you do not currently possess. "AT" means "has" in American Sign Language.

7) Stopping yourself from making the ASL sign and making a simple movement instead will help you generate negative statements (like "I don't know").

8) When you want to ask a question in American Sign Language (more on that below), just add the sign "DE" at the end of your sentence.

9) If you want to say "then" in your phrase, you can do so by using the symbol DE. For instance: (Remember, you don't have to use this with "then.")

10) Substitute passive ASL signals for the word "and" in each sentence that contains it.

11) Replace the inactive word "or" in sentences with dynamic ASL signs, like in rule number eleven.

12), Above, except with your hand down and pointing to where you want to indicate the location.

13) With your palms facing each other, draw the "space" handshape to indicate someone's name.

14) Use the sign DE before your name and then point to yourself to indicate a title such as Dr., Rev., Mr., or Mrs.

15) If you wish to point out a specific city or street, sign AT followed by the name of the place, and then point there.

16) You can also use an ASL word in place of "and" or "or" in a statement. To do this, make a question mark with your fingers, and then sign the word that best describes your response.

17) You can also use an ASL word in place of "then," "and," or "or" in a statement. More on that to come.

18) It is proper ASL grammar to sign SLAP when a phrase has the same meaning as a single ASL word.

19) Use two different Deaf people's names to construct a letter (like "s") that is part of a word.

20) It is proper grammar to insert a pause between signs when using the same sign for different purposes.

21) First, make the sign that needs to be done, and then add an ASL word after it.

Chapter 8: ASL Classifiers

Photo 1 should depict any kind of transportation, such as a car, a boat, a bicycle, etc.

Photo 2 depicts items that are long and thin.

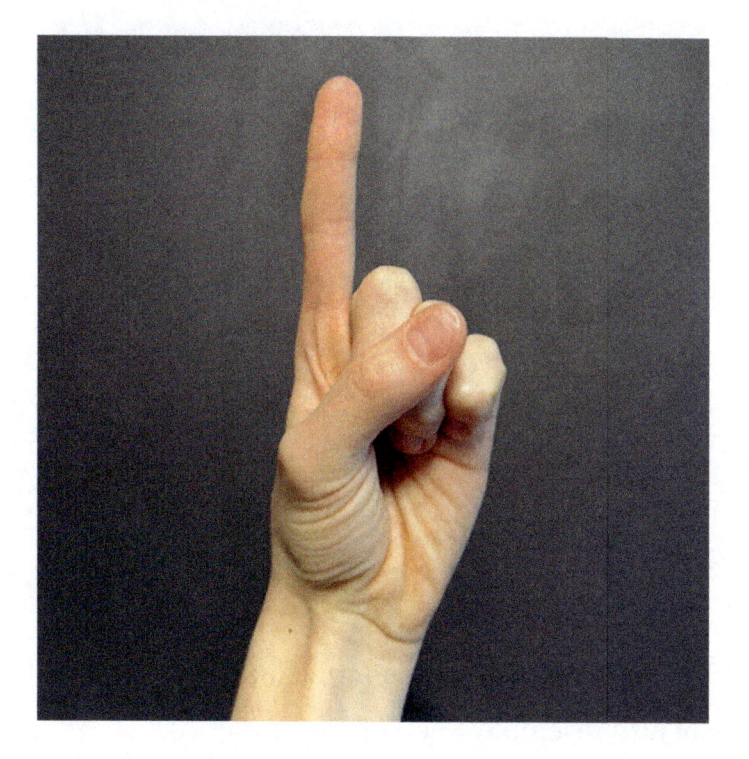

Photo 3 depicts objects with a thick cylinder shape, such as a glass or a cup.

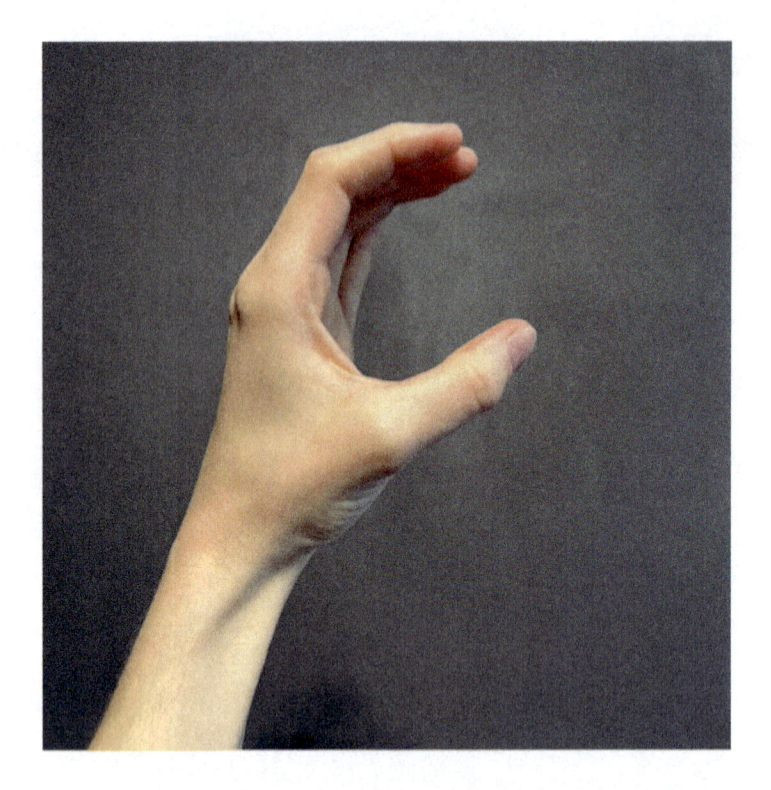

Photos 4 and 5 depict a large quantity of something (such as a crowd of people), an object (such as a snowball), or a place inside the city.

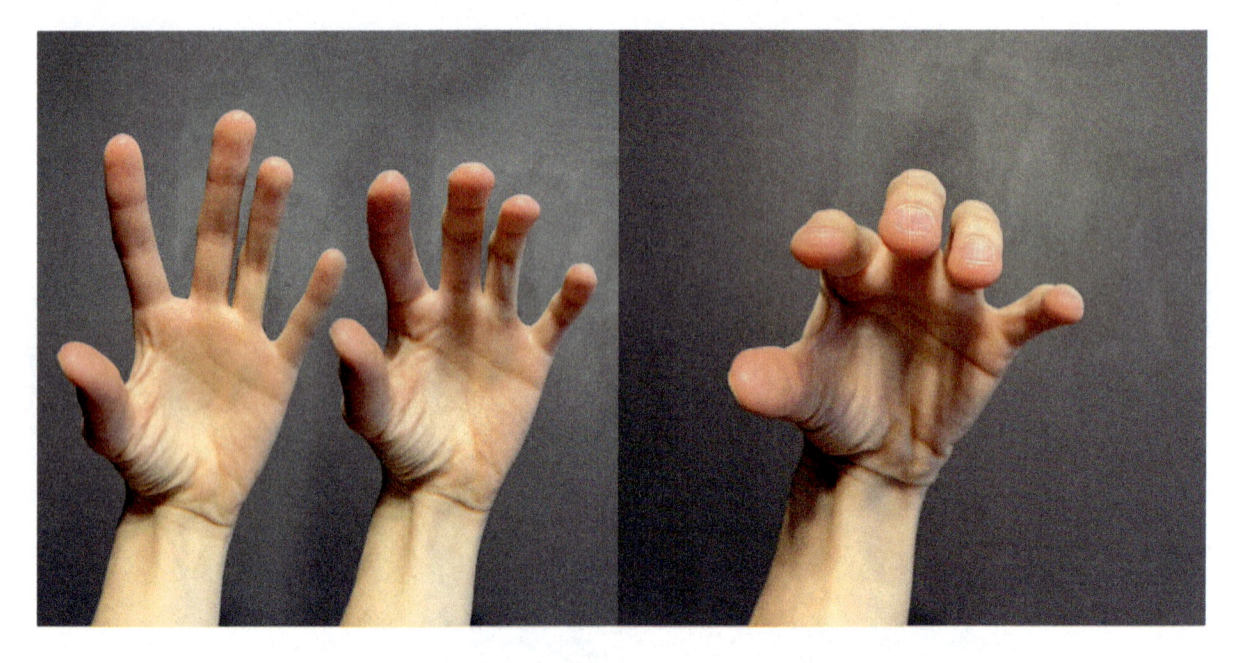

Photos 6-7 These may either depict humans (two individuals walking or sitting) or an animal in motion; if reversed, they can also resemble a person's legs.

American Sign Language

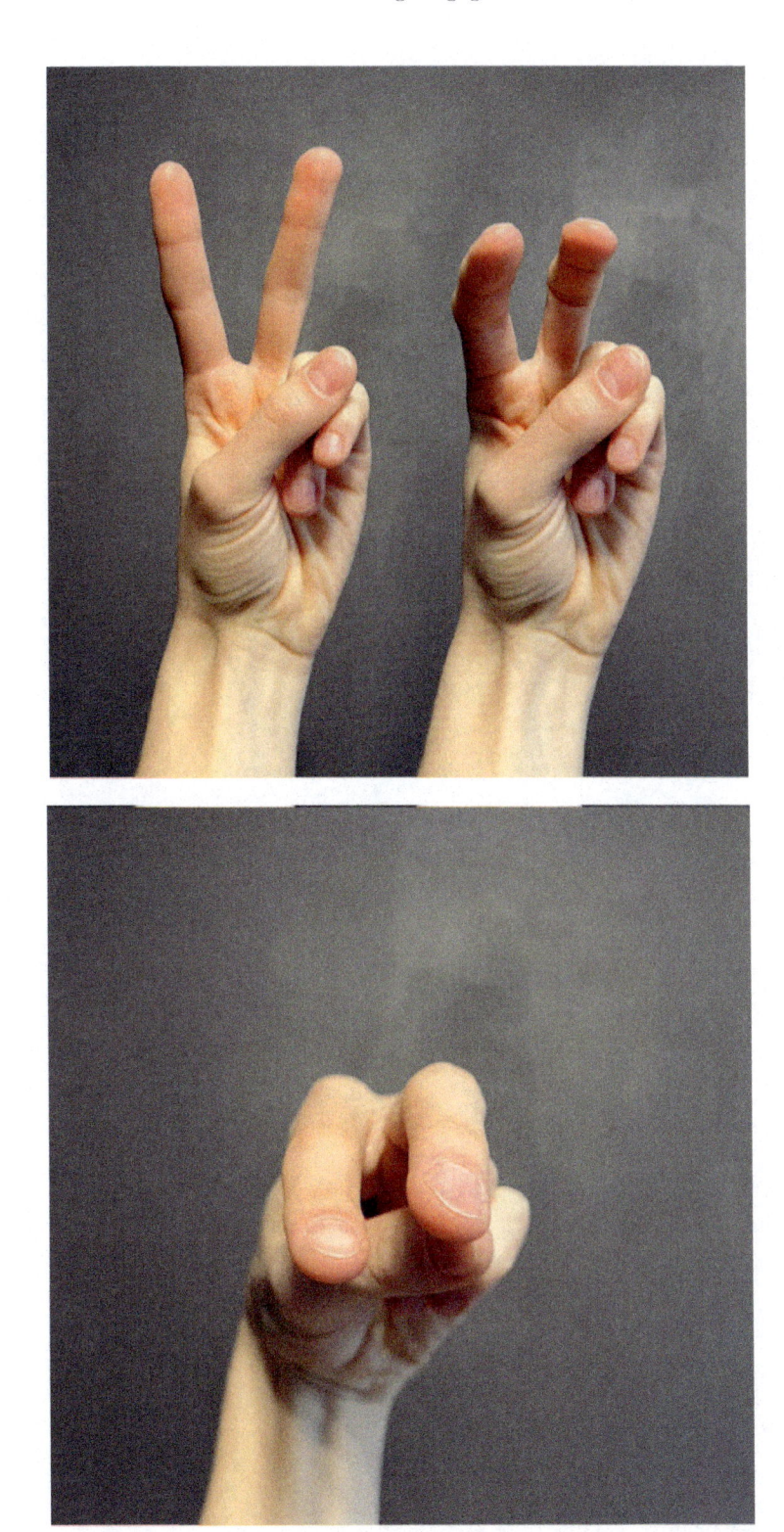

Photo 8 These represent little rectangular objects such as credit cards and cheques.

Photo 9 resembles photo 8, except it illustrates circular objects, such as dishes.

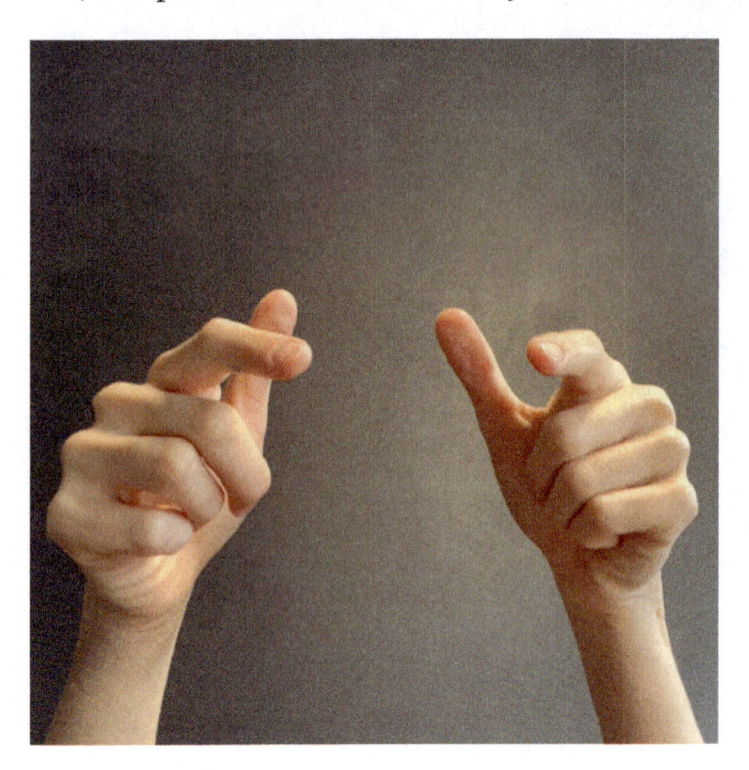

57

Photo 10 depicts something flat.

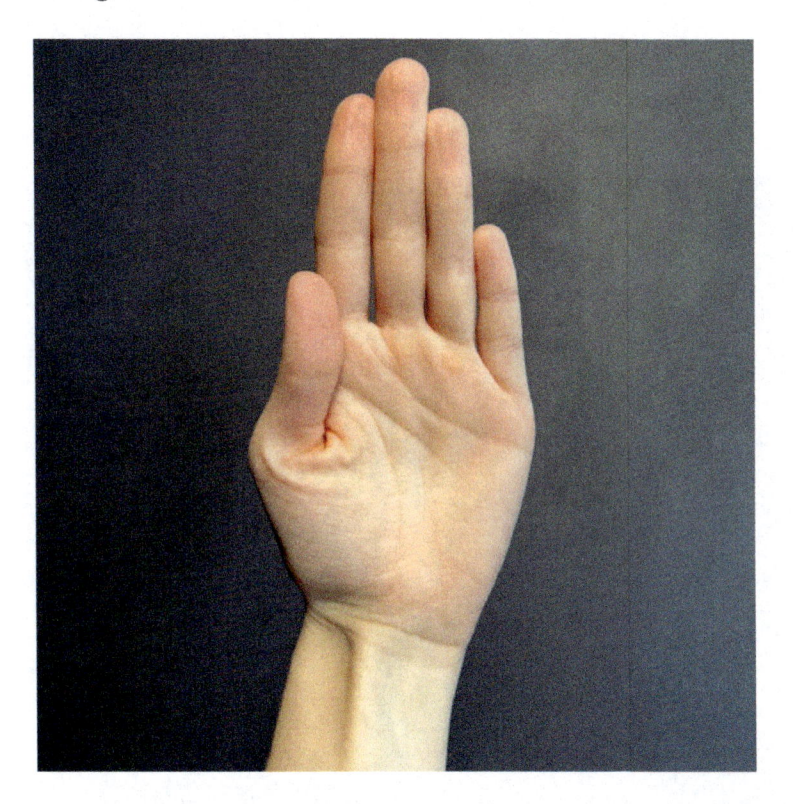

Photo 11 can convey concepts such as flowing water or curtains and individuals walking in a line.

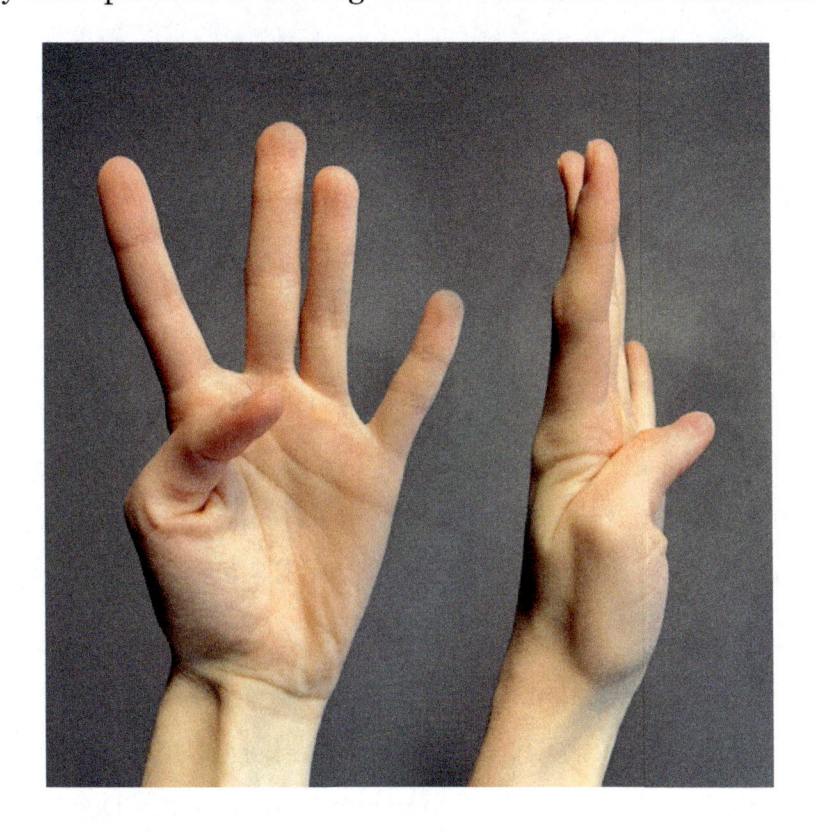

Image 12 is meant to show an item in a certain area.

Community of the deaf

The culture of people who are deaf comprises all facets of daily life for this population. Discover how to get involved, from bringing attention to important topics like audism to supporting the arts.

The American School for the Deaf was founded in Connecticut in 1817, making the state the cradle of deaf culture in the United States. The American School for the Deaf in Connecticut is credited as being the birthplace of deaf culture in the United States in 1817.

As a representation of the language community that is Deaf American Decision, American Sign Language is considered a minority language. Deaf children and a few hearing individuals who learn American Sign Language can be welcomed into the larger deaf community even though they are medically classified as deaf. On the other hand, the phrase "Deaf American" refers to solely those persons who use American Sign Language (ASL) as their main language. This includes all people who have hearing loss.

Because deafness is considered a source of positive identity and pride in deaf culture, human-centric vocabulary (such as "deaf" and "hard of hearing") has been rejected in deaf culture for a very long time. Instead, members of the deaf community refer to themselves as "deaf" or "hard of hearing" in their native language. The student who identifies as the capital letter D in the above example is the Silent student. When someone has a hearing loss, they are said to be deaf (with a lowercase d). Typically, those individuals who identify as deaf first and foremost before considering any other identification.

The activism of members of the Deaf and Hard of Hearing Community

There is a strong tradition of advocacy within the community of deaf and hard-of-hearing individuals. Students at Gallaudet University have participated in demonstrations on two separate occasions, the first time in the 1980s and the second in the early 2000s.

The first campaign, "Deaf President Now," successfully got Gallaudet University to choose its first deaf leader for the presidency. The second protest, called "Unity for Gallaudet," rallied students against a presidential candidate who was unpopular among the student body and brought attention to academic difficulties at Gallaudet.

The Development of Assistive Technology Through Time and Space

As long as there have been people with hearing loss, there has also been assistive technology. People who were previously deaf or hard of hearing can now hear, allowing them to utilize the telephone system and watch television programs for the first time.

Even though you may have the impression that closed captioning has been around for ages, the fact of the matter is that closed captioning is a very new innovation. The technology was first used in 1972 when open captioning was used on an episode of The French Chef. Subsequently, in the early 1980s, closed captioning became available, although with significant restrictions. The Telecommunications Act of 1996 made it mandatory to provide closed captioning, which is now widely accessible to persons who are deaf or hard of hearing.

Although it is a relatively new technology, the history of cochlear implants stretches back farther than those of closed captions. The very first effort to improve hearing via the use of electricity was made in the year 1790. In the latter part of the 20th century, the technology had a meteoric rise in popularity; by 1984, it had long before ceased to be considered experimental. The development of this technology is proceeding at a dizzying speed.

Hearing aids have come a long way since they resembled humorous trumpets and are now as sophisticated as BTEs.

It is easy to forget communication problems in this day and age of email, text messaging, and video chatting services like Skype; this is especially true in families with deaf parents and hearing children. However, before these improvements, there existed something called a TTY, which stands for telephone typewriter. In 1964, Robert Weitbrecht, the man who invented the teletypewriter (TTY), was the first person to use it to make a long-distance phone conversation.

Chapter 9: Common tenses to learn in American sign language.

American Sign Language uses hand signs to represent spoken words and phrases. These symbols denote a certain tense when used with the appropriate verb and noun. American Sign Language often uses the present, past, and future tenses. If you want to have a meaningful conversation with native sign language speakers, you'll need to learn about these tenses and how they're formed.

Before now

Constructing the past tense requires a movement outward from the shoulder. A circular motion is made with the extended hand. This is the accepted way to talk about things that have already happened.

Time Is Never Ending

There are two ways to express the present tense in American Sign Language. One approach is to make the same gesture as when using the past tense, but this time with the hand closed. In this alternative strategy, a "time marker" is utilized. When the fingers are spread and the palm is up, the hand is in this position.

Down the Road

In order to form the future tense, you can either mimic the past tense's pattern or use a "key word." A hand is held open and the fingers are circling upward. What you say after making these gestures is essential if you want to convey the notion that you are discussing something that will happen in the near future. If you want to signify "tomorrow," you may hold out your hand and pronounce the word. When telling a story, it's important to use these cues to show when an event took place in the past, the present, or the future.

Mandatory: In the Past

American Sign Language predominantly uses the past, present, and future tenses. Common gestures for the past tense involve a circular motion that starts at the shoulder and moves outward. A circular motion is made with the extended hand. This is the accepted way to talk about things that have already happened.

This icon denotes a person's presence at a previous epoch. The locations of the speaker are indicated by the prepositions "at" and "in".

The hand is open palm front with fingers close together and the index finger extended but without touching any of the other fingers.

Variations: The palm might be down or up when making the "was" sign, depending on the situation. The downward-facing variation is used to comment on someone's looks or emotional state. If you're telling a story about the past, use the one when the narrator looks up into the clouds.

Present Moment

There are two ways to express the present tense in American Sign Language. One approach is to make the same gesture as when using the past tense, but this time with the hand closed. The second strategy employs a "time marker," a kind of measure. The palm is facing upward in a relaxed attitude of the hand.

How to Hold Your Hands Properly Place your palms together in front of you in a prayer position, and then extend your index finger without touching the other fingers.

The "is" sign can be made in two different ways: with the palm facing down or upside down. In expressing someone's outer appearance or emotional state (a so-called "state-of-being" or "description of their state"), the reversed version is used. The forward-facing version should be used when talking about the past, especially if the event in question was a time period.

Prospective Verb Forms

Position your hand as if you were going to use the tense of the past, but then throw your fingers upward in a circular motion that leaves the ceiling free. This gesture represents the future tense. What you say after making these gestures is critical to conveying the notion that you are discussing something that will happen in the near future. Indicating the time period in which an incident took place can be useful whether you're telling a narrative set in the past, the present, or the future.

How to Hold Your Hands Properly Place your palms together in front of you in a prayer position, and then extend your index finger without touching the other fingers.

The palm can be facing down or up when making the "will" sign, depending on the situation. This version, with its lower profile, is used to comment on someone's outward look or emotional state. The forward-facing version should be used when talking about the past, especially if the event in question was a time period.

Chapter 10: Commonly Used Signs

The first chapter is dedicated to teaching the reader the fundamentals of American Sign Language. This book will show you that American Sign Language (ASL) is about more than just learning signals by guiding you through the process of communicating with deaf and hard-of-hearing persons. Numerous frequently used ASL signals and their meanings in text form are included. Keep reading to learn how to sign words and how to spot them quickly.

Facial expressions are just as important as hand gestures in any sign language, so keep that in mind. This means that eyebrow movements and other forms of body language are highly valued in interactions between people. Use these motions and gestures to give the signs you're using meaning, much as varied vocal tones and inflections provide diverse meanings to spoken words.

Keep in mind that much like spoken languages, American Sign Language has its own unique background, culture, syntax, and vocabulary. Although ASL will be entirely different from spoken languages like English, it will nonetheless have all the essential components of a language. But it does have its own peculiarities, such as its own word order conventions and its own ways of indicating certain functions. In English, for instance, the pitch of a speaker's voice rises as they shift from expressing a statement to asking a question. When asking a question in American Sign Language, users will enlarge the pupils, tilt their heads upward, and elevate their eyebrows.

People who are deaf, especially those who are completely deaf, may never hear music; consequently, signing languages are predicated on the idea that a deaf person's primary means of interacting and gaining knowledge reception is their sight, rather than their hearing. Although becoming proficient in ASL will require significant time and work, this book is the ideal place to begin.

Phrases

Learning a language's foundational phrases is the first and most important step. Increasing your vocabulary through the study of simple words is a great idea. It serves as a starting point from which progress can be made toward linguistic fluency. Learning a language like ASL is simplified with the help of these phrases, which cover topics like numbers, individuals, inquiries, families, and so on. However, it should be noted that the words and phrases included in these lists and categories are simply the tip of the iceberg when it comes to ASL.

Numbers

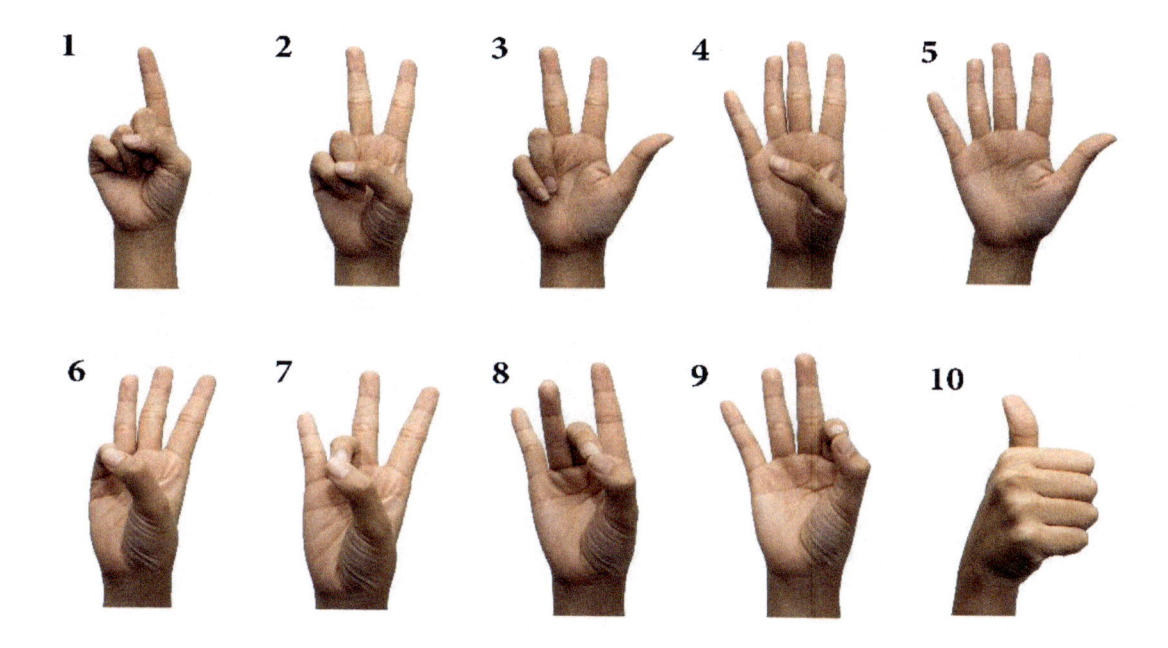

Every language relies heavily on the ability to count and use numbers in practical situations. Learning to sign the numerals 1 through 10 can help you in many areas of your life, from scheduling appointments to going to the bank. Knowing how to give someone your phone number or other numerical information in American Sign Language (ASL) might open up many options for you.

When signing a number, you must remember your palm's orientation. The first five digits require an inward-facing palm, whereas digits six through ten require an outward-facing palm. Between the ages of 11 and 15, your palm will face you, and between the ages of 16 and 19, it will face the other person in the conversation. When dealing with plurals, it is customary to indicate the item name first, then the quantity. Adding an "s" at the end of a word to make it plural in English is unnecessary in American Sign Language.

If you want to sign a number like 30, 40, or 50, you should start by signing the first digit, which would be a 3, 4, or 5, and then follow it with the sign for 0. Signing numerals in the hundreds, like 400, involves signing the number 4, then the sign for the hundred. Twisting your wrist inwards as you sign a number indicates that the number is ordinal, as in "first," "second," "third," and so on.

Time

Defining a few terms that will be utilized throughout this discussion of time in ASL is vital. Your dominant limb is the right hand and arm if you are right-handed. If you are left-handed, however, your dominant arm and hand are the opposite.

The sign for "day" is made by holding out one's minority arm (the left arm, for right-handers) in front of the body, palm down, pointing to the right. Your right elbow should be on top of your left hand, and your right arm should be pointing up. Move your right hand along an arc around your torso while keeping your right elbow above your left hand.

TIME

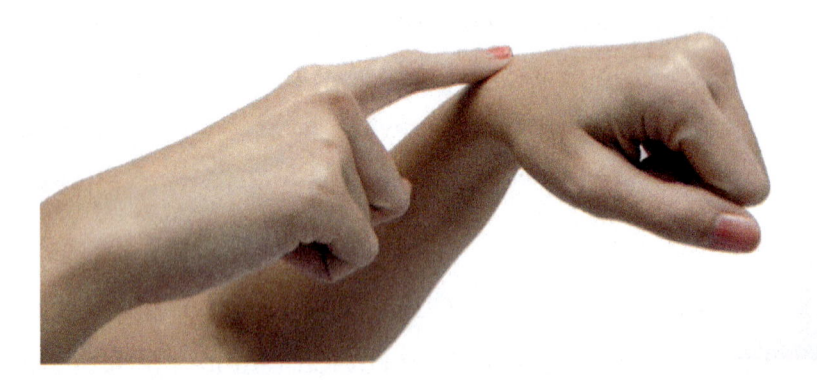

The sign for "evening" or "night" is made by holding out the non-dominant arm (often the left) horizontally with the palm of your hand facing toward the ground and the fingers pointing to the side. Next, the user will rest the index finger of their right hand on the inside of their left hand, palms facing each other, and fingers pointing down.

The sign for "week" is made by moulding the dominant hand (the right hand, in most circumstances) into an index-finger hand configuration with the tip of the index finger facing radiating and then sweeping the hand over the forearm of the hand that does not dominate (the left hand, in most cases).

The international symbol for "month" is made by pointing the middle fingers of the dominant (right) hand upwards while turning the palm of the non-dominant (left) hand backwards. The next step is to follow the left index finger's outline with the right index finger.

Straightforward, the sign for 'year' is produced by making a fist with both hands. For right-handed people, stack your fists such that your right one rests atop the left one. Then, make a fist with your right hand and rotate it around your left. Your right hand should circle your left fist before returning to its original position.

Family

By resting your thumb on your chin and spreading your fingers wide, you may make the sign for "mother." The sign for father is quite similar to the sign for mother, except that the thumb is placed on the forehead rather than the chin.

To write "boy," "male," or "a human being," make the same gesture as if you were snatching a cap and placing it on your head. To sign "girl," "female," or "woman," place the tip of your thumb on your cheek with your fingers closed. Then, move your thumb down your cheek toward your chin.

grabbing one's hands together is a universal gesture meaning "married." This indicates that the dominant right hand should rest atop the non-dominant left hand for right-handed people.

If you want to sign "baby," you can do it by placing one arm beneath the other, as if carrying a baby and then swinging your hands back and forth.

Places

To sign "home," bring your dominant hand's thumb and fingers together and touch your cheek, a little above the chin, at the side of your lips. After two inches, touch your cheek again. It's on the cheek, not the mouth.

Users make fists for "work." As both palms face down, use your dominant hand (right hand for right-handed persons) to tap the top of your non-dominant or left fist a few times.

"School" looks like clapping. Clap with your dominant hand on your non-dominant palm.

Sign "church" with your dominant hand as a "c." Place your dominant hand on top of your non-dominant fist. The dominant hand's thumb should rest on the non-dominant hand's back.

Feelings

The sign meaning "happy" is to open both hands before you and circle them forwards, down, backwards, and up once. Your hands will move together. Imagine lightly tapping or hitting your chest.

Claws are the angry symbol. Put your fingertips against your tummy and forcefully draw both claws up and outwards as if you were tearing something out. A furious face will help you communicate.

The sign meaning "sad" is two hands in front of your face, palms facing you. Then bend your head slightly forward and run both hands down your face. A sorrowful face conveys this sentiment.

Sorry, apologies, and regrets use the same sign. Make a fist with your dominant hand, thumb on top, and rotate it clockwise on your chest. Repeat this with a regretful face.

To sign "cry," place each index finger under each eye and pull it down over your cheek several times.

Touching your dominant hand's fingers to your lips and placing them in your non-dominant hand makes the "good" sign. This symbol requires palms up.

The sign for "love" is two fists crossed over the chest. If you want to sign "I love you," point to yourself, make the love sign, and then point to the person.

Common terms

Claw your dominant hand to sign "hot." Put the claw on your mouth with the thumb and fingers on the sides and slide it outward and downward quickly, like you would remove something hot from your mouth. Faster means hotter.

The sign for "cold" is shaking both fists before you as if you were shivering. Sign "very cold" with the same gesture but with more facial expressions. In the cold, hunch your shoulders and move your arms faster and tighter.

A child symbol is patting a child's head. Pretend to pat a child twice with your dominant hand. The plural "children" symbol differs. Instead of two pats on one child's head, it will look like one pat followed by a rapid right turn to pat a second youngster.

Hold the fingers of your dominant hand, such as your right, towards your lips, palms facing you, and hand open to sign "thank you." Gently glide your hand forward and down toward the person you're talking to.

Health

To sign HEALTH, raise both hands in front of your body with palms opposite toward one another in a flexible "5" form. Pull the palms of your hands out from your body's surface and form a "S" shape.

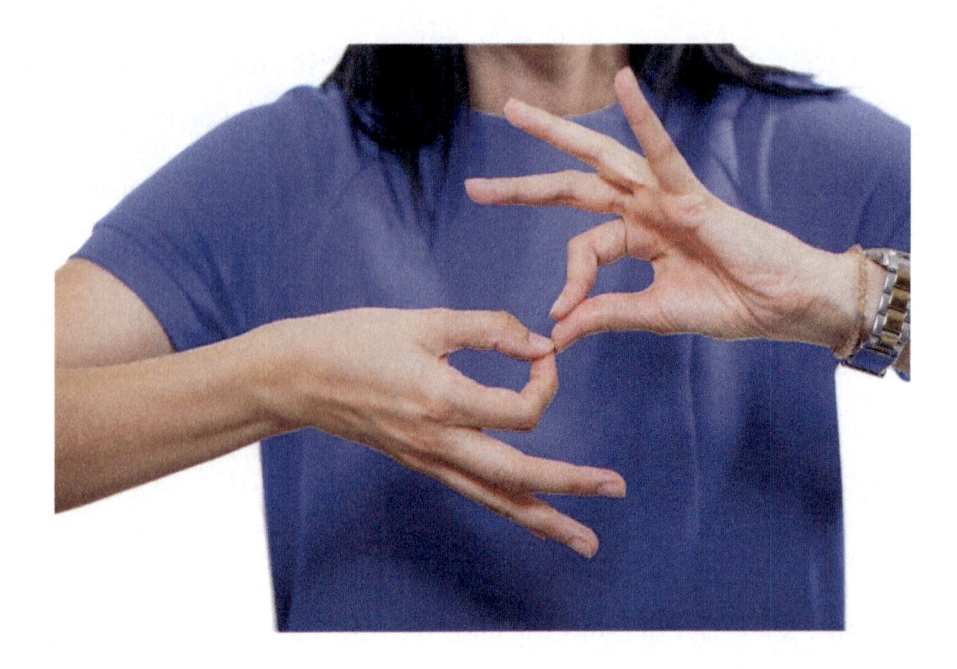

PAIN

Put your palms together to sign PAIN. Bring your index hands together and twist them oppositely. This sign can imply head, stomach, or overall pain.

SICK

Sign SICK by forming a "5" with both hands and pointing the middle fingers forward. Touch the pointed end of your middle finger to the back of your head with your dominant hand and your tummy with the hand that is not your dominant one. This indication indicates sickness.

MEDICINE

Your less-used hand has a palm-up B shape. Your dominant hand is a 5. Place your B hand's middle finger tip in the palm. Swap your dominant hand.

HEART

With the middle finger upward, the dominant hand forms a "5". Tap your index finger twice before your heart.

WASH

Palms face each other in a "A" form. Dominant hand under non-dominant. Double-tap your heart with your middle finger.

INFECTION

Position your heavier hand in a "I" near your shoulder. Shake your hands. If you don't seem disgusted, it'll imply coverage instead of infection.

ALLERGY

The sign in question is two-part. Your dominant hand contacts your nose in a "1" shape. Next, both hands form a G with their fingers pointed toward each other. Pull your dominant hand toward your non-dominant. Navigate this advertisement smoothly.

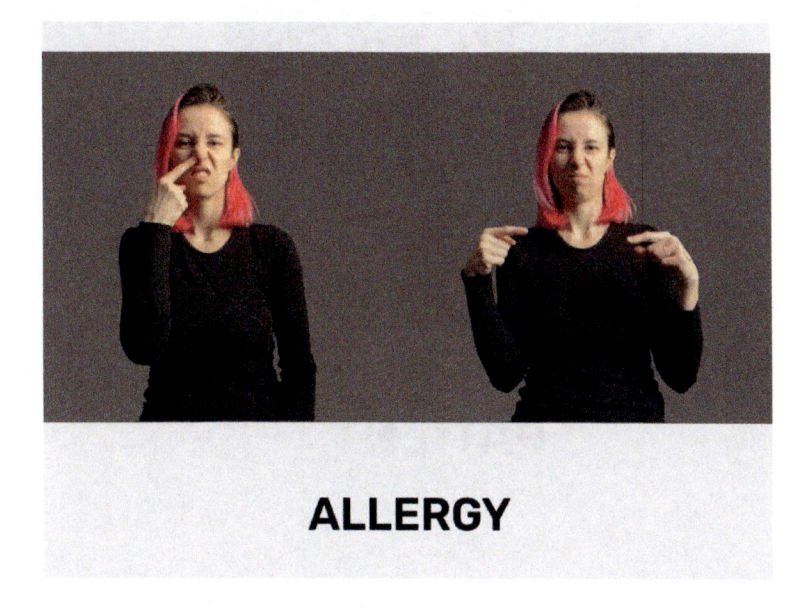

HOSPITAL

Draw a plus sign on the side of your non-dominant arm by making a H with your dominant hand.

[Image: HOSPITAL sign demonstration]

HOSPITAL

PATIENT

Put your thumbnail on your chin and drag it downward about 2 inches.

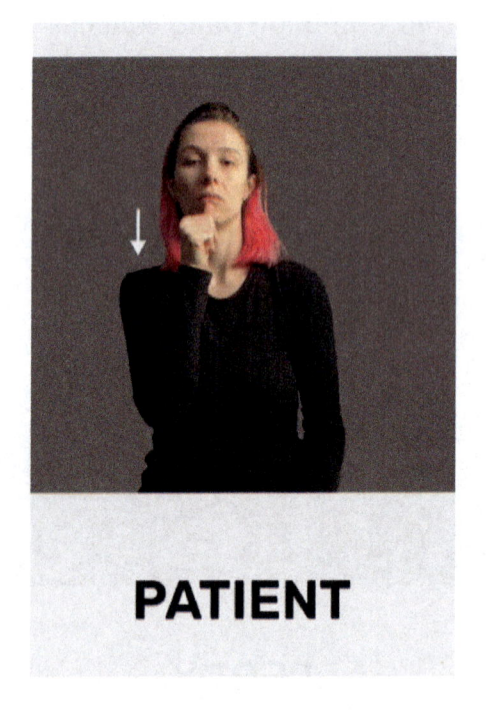

[Image: PATIENT sign demonstration]

DOCTOR

To sign "doctor," curve your dominant hand and touch the inside of the wrist of your other hand, as if you were taking a pulse. Form a letter "D" with your dominant hand and touch it to the inner wrist of your non-dominant hand. This is another way to say "doctor" in ASL.

DOCTOR

Days of the week

MONDAY

To sign "Monday," start by making an "M" shape with your dominant hand, with the palm facing towards you. Then, move your hand in a counterclockwise circle around the "M" shape.

TUESDAY

To sign "Tuesday," start by making a T shape with your dominant hand, with the palm facing towards you. Then, move your hand in a counterclockwise direction around the T shape twice.

WEDNESDAY

To sign "Wednesday," start by making a W shape with your dominant hand, with the palm facing towards you. Then, move your hand in a counterclockwise circle around the W shape.

THURSDAY

To sign "Thursday," begin by making a T shape with your dominant hand, with the palm facing towards you. Next, shoot your hand out into an H shape with the palm still facing you. Finally, make a small circle around the H shape away from your body.

FRIDAY

To sign "Friday," begin by making an "F" shape with your dominant hand, with the palm facing towards you. Next, move your hand in a counterclockwise circle around the "F" shape to make a circle.

SATURDAY

To sign "Saturday," start by making an "S" shape with your dominant hand, with the palm facing towards you. Then, move your hand in a counterclockwise circle around the "S" shape.

SUNDAY

To sign "Sunday," make an open "B" shape with both hands and hold them up in front of your body at eye level. Then, move both hands in opposite directions around the circle in a counterclockwise direction. This sign is not commonly used in sign language.

Chapter 11: Special Tips for ASL

The American Sign Language, while not all-encompassing, has recently become an extremely prevalent language. When acquiring this dialect, special precautions need to be taken, the same kind of special care, respect, and expectations that you would be confronted with when developing any other kind of foreign spoken language. It is now time to acquire some special suggestions and adhere to a few essential rules that will further assist you in comprehending and appreciating American Sign Language as an exquisite means of interpersonal interaction. Now that you are familiar with the fundamentals of ASL and have most likely been practicing the gestures that have been described in this book, it is time to acquire knowledge and some special tips and comply with some significant recommendations.

Realizing that mastering any language will need a significant investment of time is an essential part of studying American Sign Language (ASL). It could take you a few months to learn the fundamentals of American Sign Language (ASL), but it will take you years to become proficient in the language. After a few months of conversing with a deaf person, you could get the impression that you have achieved fluency in the language. However, this is not the case. What you need to remember is that it is not your fluency that allows you to have a basic discussion, but rather the fact that the deaf person is multilingual and will be capable of comprehending what you are committing, even though you fail to get it right. This is something that you ought to be aware of in order to have a productive discussion.

Practice

Practice makes perfect, as the old adage goes. Students pursuing an education in American Sign Language should take note of this. A student can become fluent in American Sign Language (ASL) if he persists in studying the language and engaging in conversation with native speakers. Any given language can be studied in a number of different methods. It's also a good idea to keep an eye out for training opportunities. Repetition and stagnation are common effects of performing the same things you've been doing from the start. Try to think of creative ways to study the language, and make ensuring you enjoy yourself!

Observing demonstrations online or in books, then implementing what you've studied with another person, are among the most fundamental ways to learn. Attending social gatherings for the deaf and even tutoring a total beginner are two examples of non-standard approaches.

Regular practice of ASL is essential if you want to enhance your fluency, accuracy, and understanding of the language.

Fingerspell

As was noted, practice is key, and fingerspelling is one particular area that you need to work on particularly. Because a sign does not exist for every word in American Sign Language, it is almost inevitable that you will need to type out some terms. It is essential to move swiftly since individuals who are fluent may do these tasks very rapidly. People who are fluent in a language will often be able to sign a word that needs to be spelled out in a sentence far more quickly than you would be able to utter the statement out loud. Practicing in front of a mirror is going to be the most beneficial thing for you to do. Construct each letter of the alphabet, and while you're at it, try your hand at some simple words. Even while learning your letters is really important, you should also teach yourself how to properly pause between words so that your sentences make sense. Because you will always need to use fingerspelling in ASL, it is critical that you develop your ability in this area.

Vocabulary

Throughout the course of this book, the significance of having a large vocabulary has been alluded to on multiple occasions. It is essential to have a sizable vocabulary whenever one is discussing any language, regardless of whether that language is spoken or signed. The use of a large vocabulary not only adds to the overall quality of our lives, but it also helps us in our personal and professional life. You may improve your everyday vocabulary by learning new signs as often as you can and practicing the signs you use on a daily basis. Practice all the signs you need every day. Not only can increasing the size of your vocabulary help you improve your communication abilities, but it will also provide you the capacity to select the words you require with a greater degree of precision. Additionally, having a large vocabulary will enable you to have a more open mind because each new term that you pick up will enable you to strengthen your thinking.

Body Language

Facial expressions and other body language are an integral elements of learning sign language, perhaps even more so than the signals themselves. American Sign Language is a highly expressive language that makes extensive use of facial expressions, body language, and hand gestures to convey meaning. In American Sign gestures (ASL), tones are represented through facial expressions and body gestures. One may determine whether two people are having a friendly chat or a heated quarrel just by watching their body language. Some indicators lack nuance without the use of facial emotions. Making and maintaining eye contact is a powerful communication tool that indicates you care about what the other person has to say. It enables you to appear as though you are contributing to the discussion.

Deaf Culture

Learning ASL requires a genuine curiosity about the deaf community. You need to be aware of the appropriate terminology to employ as well as that which may be deemed offensive or inappropriate. It's rare for deaf parents to pass on their condition to their children, thus it's crucial for hearing people to be accepting of deaf-specific institutions like schools and clubs. Maintain a low profile and demonstrate a genuine interest in learning the local language and customs.

Ask a deaf acquaintance for private instruction, or plan a get-together where everyone will use sign language exclusively. Go to a gathering of the deaf with your pals or by yourself. If you want to polish your talents, look for deaf plays or shows in your area or volunteer at a deaf school. Finding other deaf people who are willing to assist you is the only requirement. Regular interaction with the deaf community is a surefire way to become fluent in sign language.

Classes

Think about signing up for a class if you want to learn American Sign Language seriously. Locally, you can take advantage of a wide range of language-learning opportunities. These courses are not only enjoyable and useful, but they also teach you a great deal and speed up your learning curve. More and more Americans are showing an interest in learning ASL as the language's popularity rises here. Some secondary and tertiary universities in the United States even provide face-to-face ASL instruction to its students. In addition, people who are making an effort to learn ASL are warmly welcomed by ASL/Deaf organizations and associations in every state in the USA. There are many certification programs and courses that can be taken in the evening.

Consider enrolling in an online course if you worry you won't be able to devote enough time to attending in-person classes or completing a comprehensive program. There are both paid and free options available for you to take classes online. Think about getting a private ASL teacher who can accommodate your busy schedule.

Reliance on English

There is absolutely no connection between ASL and English. It is not a language that can be translated into English; rather, it is a language that is entirely independent of English and exists in its own right. If you want to be successful in learning American Sign Language, you have to be willing to give up your voice and your dependence on English. When you are trying to learn sign language, and you are seeing someone else sign, you should make an effort not to translate what you see in your thoughts. Although it may appear to be challenging at first, and in fact it will be, continuing to do so will assist you in becoming more proficient. The more proficient you become in the target language, the less likely you will feel the need to translate. A discussion with a teacher or with other students might be much more beneficial than taking notes. To better remember the language you are studying, consult various reference materials such as books, DVDs, and videos. You have to approach this whole process with the mentality that you are learning a totally new language, not something that you will utilize to improve your English language skills. Only then will you be successful. As you have most likely deduced by this point, American Sign Language possesses its own grammar, syntax, and structure.

Other tips

- The foundational knowledge you acquire early will serve you well. Starting with the signs for basic phrases like "hello," "goodbye," and "please" can get you far.

- One important distinction between ASL and other sign languages is that the verb "to be" does not exist in ASL. So instead of signing "I am going to the supermarket," you would just sign "Supermarket I go."

- The best way to learn is to observe. If you want to educate yourself independently, the internet is a fantastic resource. Practice with videos you find online.

- Going out and interacting with native speakers is essential for learning the language. Meet together with other deaf people and sign at events. Meeting new people is a great way to speed up your language acquisition.

- Remember that you're social beings, and that the reason languages exist is so that you can communicate with one another. Make use of your knowledge and communicate with others.

Practice Tips

Acquire the top 100 most useful vocabularies.

To begin speaking, you'll need to familiarize yourself with some fundamental language. That is why, in the start of your ASL adventure, you should focus on learning the fundamentals, such as "hello," "thank you," and "please." As soon as you learn a few words, you may begin conversing.

Acquaint yourself with the finger alphabet.

It is essential to learn the ASL letters when first starting out with American Sign Language. If you know the letters of the alphabet, you can sign any word. That's why it's possible to spell a sign if you can't remember it.

Spell out words like "computer" and "tree" with your fingertips to hone your finger dexterity.

Learn how to put the question "How can I signed..." in sign language.

Learn the finger letters and the phrase "How do I sign... (also known as word)?" and you'll be able to ask for any sign. So, let's look into this concept.

Conversation!

Do not wait to start talking and getting things signed. Don't be shy about reaching out to other people who use American Sign Language once you've learned the alphabet and some simple phrases. Learning a new language relies heavily on actual conversation. Many people who are learning a new language make the mistake of putting off making contact with native speakers.

Find a local Deaf community to join or a practice partner to work with.

To have a conversation, you must first find other people to talk to. There is a Deaf community in virtually every municipality. Get together with other signers and frequent events.

If you don't live near a major city, you might look for a study buddy online (e.g., through Facebook groups). Video chats between you and a friend are possible.

Make no attempt to comprehend everything.

Many students of foreign languages worry that they won't be able to communicate effectively with native speakers. You can get away with without knowing what each symbol means in a sentence. Try to get a feel for the phrases as a whole. Your skills will steadily improve, and you'll find yourself more easily grasping the material. If you're having trouble comprehending a statement or need clarification, the people you're signing with will likely be understanding and helpful.

Learn the common jargon in your field.

Learn some key phrases that hold significance for you. This will help you speak more fluidly, especially in social situations!

The learning curve varies over time, so keep that in mind.

Keep in mind that everyone experiences bad days from time to time. It's normal to feel like you've hit a wall and aren't making any headway at all on certain days. Don't fight these emotions; instead, give in to them. Contrary to popular belief, learning does not occur in a linear fashion. Even though it may be challenging at times, your skills will grow over time.

Get in the habit of doing good.

Don't forget that reliability beats out zeal any day. Get in the habit of studying ASL daily! You don't have to sit down and study for an hour every day. You can improve your skills in as little as 5-10 minutes. Try to keep it going as best you can!

Attempt to fail! Keep a carefree, youthful spirit. Let go of your need for perfection.

Young people often pick up information more quickly than adults do because they have less of a concern of making mistakes. The process of learning relies heavily on the inevitable occurrence of mistakes. However, the vast majority of people worry about their appearance and think they should avoid making mistakes. Don't bother trying not to mess up. Behaving like a child will help you acquire knowledge more rapidly. No one will ever judge you.

Utilize the 80/20 rule

Maybe you've heard of the "80/20 rule," another name for the "Pareto principle."

The Pareto principle states that around 80% of effects arise from 20% of inputs. The 80/20 rule applies to learning ASL, suggesting that the first 20% of your studies will have the most impact on your proficiency. In other words, your learning growth is largely attributable to a relatively small quantity of your learning input.

Language learning is propelled forward by the learner's active participation in the target language. The ability to read, write, and communicate effectively is crucial. Don't get mired down in grammar or vocabulary that you might never use again.

Try looking up your favorite YouTuber.

Learn ASL by diving deep into the culture and language. Find your preferred channels with the help of social media. Putting yourself in an ASL environment will help you learn faster and enjoy the process more.

Track your development.

Keeping tabs on how far along you are in your ASL studies helps motivate you to keep at it. Taking weekly videos of yourself signing is a great way to see how far you've come. You can watch the movies right away, or you can save them for later and share them online. They are a great memento of your time spent learning American Sign Language.

Establish objectives.

Motivating yourself may require setting short-term goals on a daily, weekly, or monthly basis. Here are a few examples.

- Learn to remember five signals a day.
- Hold one sign language conversation per week.
- Learn to recite twenty sentences a month.

Don't take yourself too seriously and always remember your "why."

The most important piece of guidance is this one. Don't lose your enthusiasm for studying ASL. If you aren't enjoying yourself, chances are you won't continue studying ASL. Since you are learning sign language, keep this in mind as well. Having a goal in mind will serve as a driving force while you pursue your studies.

Conclusion

The deaf community uses American Sign Language (ASL), sometimes known as the language of the deaf. While not universal, sign language is widely used among the deaf population in countries like Finland, Austria, Canada, Germany, Norway, and the United States. British Sign Language is just one of many sign languages used worldwide.

There are several compelling reasons to study this language. If you are deaf, learning American Sign Language (ASL) will make communicating with other deaf people much simpler. Being fluent in ASL will make it simple for you to integrate into Deaf culture. Even if you aren't deaf, learning sign language will be useful if you spend a lot of time with people who are. It will make the deaf people around you feel appreciated and understood and facilitate your integration into the community. Teachers in deaf schools need to know ASL to instruct their students in the language.

This language contains numerous essential words. Family names like "mom," "brother," "dad," "sister," "grandma," "grandpa," "baby," "uncle," and "aunt" are among the most meaningful. Marriage, singleness, divorce, and separation are significant terms in ASL. Words like "work," "home," "store," "school," "come," "go," "drive," "car," "night," "day," "month," "week," "year," "cold," "hot," "hamburger," "cup," "apple," "egg," "pizza," and the names of other foods should also be learned in sign language. It is also important to know how to properly use words like "pants," "shoes," "socks," "underwear," "coat," and "shirt." You should also be familiar with the words for various emotions, such as "sad," "happy," "angry," "love," "bad," "good," "sorry," and "cry." Important colours, animals, and polite request words like "please," "excuse me," and "thank you" should also be learned. The phrases "nice," "clean," "sleep," "bathroom," "hurt," and "wash" are also useful to know.

Learning accurate fingerspelling is also an important part of developing fluency in American Sign Language. If you want to learn how to spell using only your fingertips, you need to do a lot of practice. If you want to avoid confusing your reader, try to avoid bouncing your hand too often.

Learning the deaf culture is essential for integrating into the deaf community with ease and success. Learn American Sign Language since it is this culture's greatest gift. Read up on the subject, watch some shows, listen to some music, and joke about to get a full grasp of deaf culture. Knowing the proper etiquette for talking with a deaf person will help you avoid any awkward situations. Read these guidelines to make communicating with the deaf easier. Do not mix the rules of the deaf culture with those of the hearing culture; the two are completely different.

Printed in Great Britain
by Amazon